Radical Tendencies in the Reformation:

Divergent Perspectives

edited by
Hans J. Hillerbrand

VOL. IX
SIXTEENTH CENTURY ESSAYS & STUDIES

Habent sua fata libelli

Volume IX

of

Sixteenth Century Essays & Studies

Hans J. Hillerbrand, Editor

Charles G. Nauert, Jr., General Editor

This book is brought to you with the generous support of
the International Research and Exchanges Board (IREX)
of Princeton, New Jersey
and
Northeast Missouri State University

Library of Congress Cataloging-in-Publication Data
Radical tendencies in the Reformation: divergent perspectives / edited
by Hans J. Hillerbrand.
    p. 140 (Sixteenth century essays & studies; v. 9)
    Includes bibliographical references and index.
    A collection of essays presented at a colloquy held under the sponsor-
ship of the annual Sixteenth Century Studies Conference in St.
Louis, October 24-26, 1986.
    ISBN 0-940474-09-3 : $25.00
    1. Anabaptists–Congresses. 2. Reformation–Congresses. 3. Radical-
ism–Congresses. I. Hillerbrand, Hans Joachim. II. Series.
BX4929.5.H55 1987   87-27383
284'.3–dc19   CIP

Designed by RUS   Cover Design by Teresa Wheeler
Printed by Edwards Brothers, Ann Arbor, Michigan
Text is set in Bembo II

∞

Contents

Jan van Leyden
From single-leaf woodcut by Erhard Altdorfer

Preface

This is a striking collection of essays. It grew out of the participation of four historians from the German Democratic Republic in a colloquy on "Radical Currents in the Reformation," which was held under the sponsorship of the annual Siteenth Century Studies Conference in St. Louis, October 24-26, 1986. While this was not the first visit of Early Modern European historians from the German Democratic Republic to the United States, the colloquy provided the setting for the first systematic exposure of American scholars of the sixteenth century to the understanding of radical tendencies in the Reformation of the sixteenth century by historians from the German Democratic Republic.

The visit took place under the auspices of the joint USA-GDR Commission on Exchange in the Humanities, which is sponsored by the International Research and Exchanges Board (IREX) of Princeton, New Jersey, and the Ministerium für Hoch- und Fachschulwesen of the German Democratic Republic. The Commission, chaired by Dr. Harry Woolf of the Institute for Advanced Studies in Princeton, designated the Reformation Era as one of the areas of emphasis. The objective was to bring together historians from the German Democratic Republic and the United States for the discussion of a common topic so as to illustrate the communality as well as divergence of historical scholarship in the two countries. Since historical scholarship in the German Democratic Republic is characterized, of course, by its adherence to the Marxist understanding of the historical process, its dialogue with American historical scholarship, which embraces a variety of approaches, raises not only questions of specific emphasis but also of divergent ideological perspectives.

The first joint activity was held in the German Democratic Republic in 1983 in the setting of the Luther anniversary that year. It was an informal colloquium of historians and church historians from the two countries and focused on the Marxist interpretation of Martin Luther.

In 1985 an agreement was reached to organize a colloquium in the United States on "radical currents of the Reformation." Historians in the German Democratic Republic are engaged in exploring the ramifications of the concept of the "Early Bourgeois Revolution" for the radicalism of the Reformation, while in the United States a lively "revisionist" debate about the Radical Reformation is currently taking place.

The original intention was to have historians of the German Democratic Republic and from the United States address identical topics. The papers were not so much to offer new research or analysis as to summarize creatively the current scholarly consensus, thereby allowing a comparative judgment as to the concerns and perspectives of each side. This approach proved not possible. Given the research priorities of the individual scholars, more individualistic topics emerged.

The organizing of the colloquy proved to be complicated and could not have been brought to fruition without the support of a number of individuals to whom deep appreciation is due. I wish to record my appreciation to my colleagues from this country and from the German Democratic Republic who were unfailingly understanding, cooperative, and helpful. Their willingness to modify personal research priorities helped make the colloquium a success.

A public word of appreciation is also due the staff of IREX for its support, including the publication subsidy for the seven papers. Vivian Abbott and Margit Serenyi of IREX were understanding enablers of a complicated project.

Helen Nader, the President of the Sixteenth Century Studies Conference, saw the creative potential of the dialogue by providing a place for the several sessions on the program of the annual conference in 1986. Finally, last by no means least, the creative competence of Bob Schnucker made the publication of the papers a pleasant experience. And this all the more, since all seven participants submitted their finished papers on time. Ms. Jeni Umble's skills produced a perfect manuscript. It should be noted the contributions of Hoyer, Laube, Looß, and Vogler reached me in English translation; however, I felt it appropriate to make certain changes to improve smoothness of style and clarity of expression.

Even a casual perusal of the seven papers will quickly indicate that many desiderata and uncertainties remain in the study of the radical currents of the Reformation. I very much hope that the dialogue represented in these papers will prove to be a catalyst for further exploration and research.

Hans J. Hillerbrand

Dallas, Texas
May, 1987

Introduction

The "radicals" of the Reformation of the sixteenth century have intrigued observers ever since the early years of the Reformation itself, when several *neue zeyttung* depicted the story and fate of Thomas Müntzer. While receiving nowhere near the attention paid to Luther or Calvin, and their respective traditions, a goodly amount of preoccupation with "radical" manifestations of the Reformation has, indeed, been characteristic ever since then. Most of this attention—though by no means all—has been blatantly negative. The "radicals" of the Reformation were meant as a horror story of both personal and theological failings.

As two of the essays of this volume point out, a great deal of lively research on "radical" forms of the Reformation has characterized twentieth century historical and theological scholarship. This research has focused on certain conceptual questions by asking how the inner cohesiveness of the seemingly bewildering variety of sixteenth century Reformation dissent and its relationship to the mainstream Reformation are to be understood. At the same time, there has also been lively monographic research into the events and persons pertaining to the radical side of the Reformation.

For both European and American scholarship, the incisive questions and considerations have been theological ones. Accordingly, the term "radical" was, as a rule, defined, in theological terms, specifically in terms of the theological relationship of a figure to Martin Luther. Recent scholarship has severely challenged this approach and argued that the "radicals" of the Reformation must be understood *sui generis* without recourse to Luther or any other reformer.

Recent scholarship has been characterized by two important developments. One has been a "revisionist" approach to the history of Anabaptism as delineated by Harold S. Bender and Robert Friedmann who were at great pain to define the movement as very much divorced from all revolutionary tendencies in the early Reformation. A second element is the provocative interpretation of the Reformation of the sixteenth century by Marxist historians. We must note that historians from the German Democratic Republic coined and employed the term "Early Bourgeois Revolution" to argue that the early German Reformation and the German Peasants' War were the dual manifestations of an early bourgeois repudiation of medieval feudalism. It was a "revolution" because it repudiated the existing social order. It was "early bourgeois" in contradistinction to the French Revolution in which the bourgeois reaction against feudalism found its final expression. While this historiography has paid much attention to the mainstream Reformation—including, recently, Martin Luther—little has been said to date about the Radical Reformation, even though it is clear that "radical" or Radical Reformation must be defined in relationship to the Early Bourgeois Revolution.

The four essays in this volume by historians from the German Democratic Republic offer a succinct summary of current Marxist historiography as it pertains to Reformation radicalism. It is delineated various ways. Adolf Laube delineates a broad sweep of historiography and assessment. A learned paper, it offers rich historiographical insight and thoughtful reflection. The other papers treat specific monographic topics: Sigrid Looß deals with the theology of the early Karlstadt, Siegfried Hoyer analyzes radical themes in the lay preaching of the early Reformation, while Günter Vogler discusses the political ramifications of the Anabaptist Kingdom in Münster.

The three contributions of the American scholars parallel those contributions. Hans Hillerbrand summarizes the rise of Reformation radicalism, Eric Gritsch tackles the familiar theme of Luther and Müntzer, while James Stayer offers reflections on Anabaptism in Münster.

The intent of the volume is to bring together current scholarship on the radical currents of the Reformation, written from different viewpoints. Each essay offers useful perspectives.

Radicalism as a Research Problem in the History of Early Reformation

Adolf Laube

THE TERM "RADICAL REFORMATION"has been used in scholarship ever since the publication of George H. Williams' monumental monograph,[1] though the term, rather than his underlying concept, has been accepted. Exclusively based on theological criteria, Williams' distinction between the "restitution" of the radicals undertaken without the support of government, on the one hand, and the government-supported "reformation" of Protestants and reform Catholics, on the other hand, together with his classification and systematization of the radicals into the different strands of Anabaptists, Spiritualists, and Evangelical Rationalists, continues to be preferred in American church historical scholarship, but it was accepted neither by Marxist[2] nor by non-Marxist[3] social historians. Prior to the publication of Williams' book, two historians from the German Democratic Republic, Günther Mülpfordt[4] and Alfred Meusel,[5] had employed the terms "radical reformation," "reformation radicals," and "radical reformation camp," but had offered substantially different definitions than did Williams. Apart from the use of the same terms, but with different semantics, there also was a certain convergence of opinion on substance and methodology, but with different terminological designations, as by Heinold Fast[6] who, with reference to Roland H. Bainton, spoke of the "left wing of the Reformation" and understood by it Anabaptists, Spiritualists, Enthusiasts (*Schwärmer*) and Antitrinitarians. The ensuing debate over terminology (Radical Reformation, or Left Wing of the Reformation, or Nonconformists, etc.) appeared to focus on marginalia. In essence, the discussion

---

[1]George H. Williams, *The Radical Reformation* (Philadelphia: Westminster, 1962).

[2]See especially Günter Vogler, "Gab es eine radikale Reformation: Bemerkungen zur Konzeption von G. H. Williams," *Wissenschaftliche Zeitschrift der Karl-Marx-Universität Leipzig* 14 (1965): 3.

[3]See, for example, Claus-Peter Clasen, *Anabaptism. A Social History 1525-1618* (Ithaca: Cornell University Press, 1972), Hans-Jürgen Goertz, Introduction to *Radikale Reformatoren: 21 biographische Skizzen von Thomas Müntzer bis Paracelsus*, ed. Hans-Jürgen Goertz (Munich, 1978); idem, *Die Täufer. Geschichte und Deutung* (Munich, 1980); Rainer Wohlfeil, *Einführung in die Geschichte der deutschen Reformation* (Munich, 1982).

[4]Günter Mühlpfordt, "Radikal–eine Kategorie in Anwendung auf Reform, Reformation und Revolution," *Reform-Reformation-Revolution*, ed. Siegfried Hoyer (Leipzig, 1980), especially 164ff and the titles cited there concerning studies by Mülpfordt in the 1950s.

[5]Alfred Meusel, *Thomas Müntzer und seine Zeit* (Berlin, 1952).

[6]Heinold Fast, *Der linke Flügel der Reformation. Glaubenszeugnisse der Täufer, Spiritualisten, Schwärmer und Antitrinitarier* (Bremen, 1962).

centered on methodological differences between theologically oriented church history and social history, as expressed by the controversies precipitated by a paper by Hans-Jürgen Goertz presented at the Sixteenth Century Studies Conference in 1978,[7] on the one hand, and by the ideological-methodological controversies between Marxist and non-Marxist scholarship, on the other hand.

However, a constructive rapprochement is obvious. Increasingly, theological and church-historical research, for instance, recognizes—notably in connection with the studies published on the occasion of the five hundredth anniversary of Martin Luther—that an exclusively theological interpretation of the Reformation is not sufficiently conclusive and that the Reformation can only be fully understood within the context of social causes and effects. Conversely, Marxist historians now recognize that theology and belief did not simply reflect social issues within the conflicts of the Reformation, but had their own relative importance. These historians accept that questions of human existence were expressed in the search for the proper way to salvation. As regards the Radical Reformation, church-historical scholarship had to give up its single-minded emphasis on the Anabaptists or Spiritualists and their separation from revolutionary movements and had to recognize that impulses for Anabaptism emerged not only from Zwingli, Humanism, and late-medieval mysticism, but also from Karlstadt and Müntzer. The Anabaptists were therefore the legitimate children of the early Reformation movement and the Peasants' War, a view long held in Marxist historiography.[8] Today all the personalities and groupings "left" of Luther are, by and large, subsumed under the term "radical" Reformation, ranging from the Zwickau Prophets and Karlstadt, Strauß, Müntzer, the Anabaptists and Spiritualists, to the Anti-trinitarians. For all that, we are still far from a commonly accepted interpretation, since monographic research has shown that the criteria underlying the summary systematizations did not characterize the entire phenomenon. Claus-Peter Clasen, Hans-Jürgen Goertz, and Klaus Deppermann[9] must be credited for guiding non-Marxist scholarship in this direction and also orienting it towards specific monographic research.

A more detailed analysis of the problem of radicalism indicates that "radical" does not so much refer to a substantive content as to an adjectival quality,

---

[7]See Hans-Jürgen Goertz, "History and Theology: A Major Problem of Anabaptist Research Today," *Mennonite Quarterly Review* 53 (1979): 177-88, as well as the responses of Carter Lindberg, John S. Oyer, William Klassen, Kenneth R. Davis, Werner O. Packull, and James M. Stayer, ibid., 189-218. The contribution by Goertz in revised form also in *Die Täufer*, 146-60.

[8]See Gerhard Zschäbitz, *Zur mitteldeutschen Wiedertäuferbewegung nach dem großen Bauernkrieg* (Berlin, 1958).

[9]Hans J. Hillerbrand, *The World of the Reformation* (New York: Scribners, 1973), 58ff; Klaus Deppermann, *Melchior Hoffman. Soziale Unruhen und apokalyptische Visionen im Zeitalter der Reformation* (Göttingen, 1979); Clasen, *Anabaptism*; Goertz, *Radikale Reformatoren* and *Die Täufer*. See also James M. Stayer, *Anabaptists and the Sword*, 2d ed., (Lawrence, Ks.: Coronado Press, 1976).

in other words, to a thoroughly consistent pursuit of a matter that seeks to go to the very roots (*radix*). This is not changed by the use of the term as a noun, as 'radicality,' 'radicalness,' 'radicalism,' since it always requires a concrete reference. In our case, the reference is the Reformation.

In order to give processes, ideas, personalities, and currents of the Reformation the label "radical," it is necessary to arrive at an understanding about the concept of the Reformation. Here a distinction should be made between two semantic levels, namely the level of historical sources and the level of scholarly analysis. The former, which is primarily concerned with the exploration of the conceptual understanding held by contemporaries, has been extensively explored in monographic literature.[10] Briefly, the studies show that the notion of Reformation was associated with the expectation of fundamental change in church and society. Based on the conviction that social and ecclesiastical conditions were deeply depraved and no longer in accord with the will of God, and thus in need of renewal in root and branch, the yearning for "reformation" was associated with the idea of a return to the idealized conditions of early Christianity and the church of the Fathers. However, this yearning—and this must be especially emphasized with regard to theological and church-historical views which see in the Reformation exclusively an attack on the existence of the church and a renewal movement of church and faith—had never been restricted to the church but had also embraced ideas about the need for change of secular social conditions. And another point needs to be stressed. The ideas about changes to be achieved through such a "reformation" varied greatly. The social forces voicing a desire for reform did not interpret "reformation" in a uniform manner, such as the pursuit of the proper way to salvation, but according to their social position and their particular self-interest. The *Reformatio Sigismundi*, the humanist and prophetic literature, the so-called Upper-Rhine Revolutionary, the Piper of Niklashausen, the adherents of the *Bundschuh*, the *Devotio Moderna*, and many others in the pre-Reformation period associated different expectations with the yearning for reform. Luther, Zwingli, and the South German reformers, Karlstadt, Müntzer, various Anabaptists and Spiritualists, Calvin, and the insurgent peasants called for "reformation" and saw themselves as its tool. And they regarded theirs as the true Reformation.

The concept of Reformation on the semantic level of scholarly analysis is somewhat more difficult to define. Rainer Wohlfeil was altogether correct when he noted that "any conceptual understanding . . . is connected with a conscious or unconscious broad notion concerning the meaning of history." "The fundamental diversity of particular cognitive efforts which are based on theoretical notions concerning history means that a possibly comprehensive

---

[10]See Eike Wolgast, "Reform, Reformation," in *Geschichtliche Grundbegriffe*, ed. O. Brunner et al., vol. 5 (Stuttgart, 1984), 13-60.

and exhaustive definition of the notion of Reformation is ruled out by a comparative technique in the sense of a pluralistic overview of different patterns of explanation."[11] This means that the term 'Reformation,' as all the other historically based concepts, is largely dependent upon an ideological-methodological standpoint. In this way it is hardly possible for it to reach general consensus. In the interest of providing mutual access to one understanding it seems to be indispensable in the scholarly discussion to indicate one's own approach.

This can be done, of course, only in a very brief and thus vulnerable fashion.[12] According to my conceptual understanding, "Reformation" is a complex notion, which refers not only to church and creed, but also to qualitative societal changes in social, ethical, and political aspirations which accompanied the attack on the church. It is a concept which, unlike the terms 'reform' and 'revolution,' cannot claim universality for the analysis of social changes in all epochs, but was coined in terms of the specifics of the time and, at any rate, cannot be replaced by the terms 'reform' or 'revolution.' To determine its specifics it is necessary to proceed from the conditions and events in the country of origin of the Reformation, i. e. from the events in Germany (*Reich*). Later adaptations, once the fundamental breakthrough in the *Reich* had occurred and a permanent inroad into the power of the Roman Church had been made, were modified because of different conditions or were only partially effective.

Based on the conditions in the Empire four incisive characteristics were, in my judgment, operative:

1. The existence of a deep societal crisis which resulted from the internal disintegration of feudalism and also from the hypertrophic blossoming of early capitalism, i.e. to use the language of the theory of formations, from the beginning transition from feudalism to capitalism. This crisis was substantially aggravated by the societal role of the Roman Church, by the manifestations of its internal decline and the decline of authority at the top. Unlike the Western European monarchies which resolved similar or identical problems by a powerful king, all attempts at reform in the *Reich* failed due to a peculiar constellation of forces. Both the eagerness of ruling forces for reform, precipitated by the prevailing crisis, and the anti-feudal opposition movement joined in the call for "reformation." The spectrum of goals initially pursued was

---

[11]Wohlfeil, *Einführung in die Geschichte der deutschen Reformation*, 44.

[12]I elaborated these questions in greater detail in a contribution, "Überlegungen zum Reformationsbegriff," in *Reformation und Revolution*, ed. Franklin Kopitzsch and Rainer Postel which is scheduled for publication in 1987. See also Adolf Laube, "Die Reformation als soziale Bewegung," *Zeitschrift für Geschichtswissenschaft* 33 (1985): 424-41.

extensive but focused on criticism of Rome and the church. Thus the Reformation grew out of a particular crisis situation, when no societal force was able to solve the urgent problems, notably the structural problems of the old order related to the church. The questions were no longer solely those of internal reforms of the feudal system, though not yet those of a revolutionary change of form.

2. Because the entire social order derived its theoretical legitimacy largely from religious-theological notions and because the church, holding a monopoly of that ideology, established itself as the force that guaranteed order, any societal change required theological support in order to challenge the authority of the church. However intense the preparation of Humanism, the *Devotio moderna*, conciliarism, and other reform movements, these neither reached the theological core of the dominant world view, nor would and could they mobilize the masses against the old powers. It is a characteristic feature of the Reformation that by resorting to the final and supreme authority, the Word of God, it questioned the existing societal conditions and thereby gained revolutionary thrust.

3. The presence of a mass basis. It is futile to speculate what might have happened to Luther had he not found enormous support among the common people. Apart from his own personal motivation that was religiously inspired, he provided theological legitimization for the changes desired by diversified social forces. Conversely, Luther needed broad support to assert himself against the Roman Church without suffering the fate of Wycliff, Hus, and many others. It was only this broad social support that turned Luther's theology into the Reformation. The concept of Reformation assumes an importance by encompassing inner-feudal reform efforts and an anti-feudal revolutionary movement, yet only the latter distinguished the Reformation from mere church reform. Any concept of Reformation which ignores this aspect and proceeds from the subsequent "reformations" in Scandanavia and England, or from the reform currents in Eastern and Southeastern Europe, fails to recognize that these reforms and reform efforts were based on the results of the Reformation in the Empire (including Switzerland). The concept of Reformation cannot be detached from the historical processes and contents in its country of origin; only these provide a yardstick for the applicability of the concept to related processes in other countries.

4. In the final analysis, the Reformation was bound to include a set of bourgeois ideas capable of promoting the process of the transformation of feudalism into capitalism. This set of ideas became evident, for example, in the new social and work ethic in connection with the struggle against begging, in the ideological delineation of forms of bourgeois living and management, in the importance of education, in the creation of a "cheap" church, in the secularizations, etc. This is the rational essence of the Weber Thesis on the correlation between Protestantism and capitalism.

All in all, the Reformation so defined is a constituent part of what is understood by Marxist historiography of the German Democratic Republic as Early Bourgeois Revolution,[13] without being fully identical with it.

Returning to our original theme, the question is what does "radical" mean in this context. The Reformation was radical to the extent to which it resulted in a revolutionary upheaval or awakening. Therefore Luther–the person who initiated the revolution–was radical at least until the time of his stay at the Wartburg. His doctrine of justification by faith alone eliminated the church as the mediator between man and God. His early concept of the church, delineated in the sacramental writings of 1519 and 1520 as well as in the *Babylonian Captivity*, portrayed the church as an invisible community of believers, a Christian community created by the preaching of the Word of God alone. The church as a legally constituted and hierarchically structured institution was rejected in principle. This was complemented by Luther's view of the priesthood of all believers as formulated at the same time in his *Open Letter to the Christian Nobility*. Luther eliminated the category of priest of the Catholic Church with his *character indelebilis* and his specific status. All of his early ecclesiology was radical in that it deprived the Roman Church of its foundations for dogmatic understanding and self-identity. His political appeals were radical as well; for example, his *Open Letter to the Christian Nobility* and his pamphlet against Prierias demanded the removal of the papal church by force, and his remark that he wanted to wash his hands in the blood of the 'Romelings'–the sympathizers with Rome. The basis for all this has to be seen in Luther's radical biblicism which allowed only the Bible as authority–and this according to the interpretation of the individual, not according to the exegesis of pope and church. This is not the place to explore the question of continuity and change in Luther's views or to ask which views remained constant over time and where Luther dissociated himself from his early views. At any rate, Luther's significance for the ensuing movement should not be measured against his views of political authority, against his later pamphlets directed against insurrection or rebellion, against his attitude in the Peasants' War and against his later approval for the establishment of the *Landeskirchen*. In his pamphlets which triggered the Reformation, especially in his main pamphlets of 1520, Luther proved to be more radical than many a so-called radical of the later period. In his radical negation of the papal church and the theological justification of this negation Luther surpassed all previous and

---

[13]For a description of the Early Bourgeois Revolution in a summarized form see Adolf Laube et al., *Illustrierte Geschichte der deutschen frühen Revolution*, 2d ed. (Berlin, 1982); Adolf Laube et al., *Deutsche Geschichte: Die Epoche des Übergangs vom Feudalismus zum Kapitalismus*, Vol. 3 (Berlin/Köln, 1983). A selection from the rich literature on the emergence and validation of the concept of the Early Bourgeois Revolution was compiled by me in the forthcoming "Überlegungen zum Reformationsbegriff." See there especially nn 2, 4, and 61. In the meantime see also Max Steinmetz, ed., *Die frühbürgerliche Revolution in Deutschland, Studienbibliothek DDR-Geschichtswissenschaft*, vol. 5 (Berlin, 1985).

many later critics of the church. He also opened the door for radical interpretations because of his socio-ethical views and desire for social reform, as expressed in his *Open Letter to the Christian Nobility* and his pamphlets *Against Usury*.[14]

Another question is (and I hesitate to answer it) to what extent the label 'radical' could also be applied to the Zwinglian and South-German Reformation. On the one hand, it has been claimed that in Zwingli—much more than in Luther—the worldly-societal aspect, the bourgeois element, and the political situation played a greater role, and that in Zwingli more far-reaching formulations of the right to resistance against tyrannical authorities are to be found. However, in my view, these differences between Zwingli and Luther seem to be characterized by different urban environments, rather than by a greater measure of radicality. In addition, the chronological sequence must be considered. The Zwinglian and the South-German Reformation gained full momentum only after differentiations began to surface in the central regions of the Lutheran Reformation. These were differentiations brought on by "radicals" wanting either to implement Luther's reforms consistently or even surpass them. Following the attack against the priests in Erfurt and the Wittenberg disturbances, Luther distanced himself from the consequences of his teachings.

This illustrates that 'radical' is a relative term. In revolutionary periods, in particular, it is subject to rapid change. What was radical at the point of departure, quickly turns into norm. It is "moderated" and becomes the basis for new demands. The specifics of the topic "Radical Reformation" are thus aimed at the groupings that were formed after the decline of the originally relatively uniform movement of Luther and anti-Roman character and turned away from the Zwinglian and South-German Reformation. It should be repeated that some of them had never reached Luther's radicality in several respects (e.g. break with the theological tradition or early ecclesiology).

After 1521/22 radicalism meant for a while the consistent implementation of Luther's efforts, if necessary by violent action, as was demonstrated by the Erfurt "storm against the priests"[15] and the Wittenberg disturbances.[16] Yet at the same time it entailed the pursuit of basically new approaches going beyond Luther, as in Thomas Müntzer at Zwickau and later especially in the

[14]See Gerhard Brendler, *Martin Luther. Theologie und Revolution* (Berlin, 1983); Adolf Laube, "Martin Luther und die frühbürgerliche Revolution," *Sitzungsberichte der Akademie der Wissenschaften der DDR. Gesellschaftswissenschaftl. Klasse 12* (1984): 32-42.

[15]U. Weiß, "Das Erfurter Pfaffenstürmen 1521: 'Haec Lutheranorum adversus Clericos seditio,'" *Jahrbuch für Geschichte des Feudalismus 3* (1979): 233-79.

[16]See Ulrich Bubenheimer's recent "Luthers Stellung zum Aufruhr. Die frühen Wurzeln des landesherrlichen Kirchenregiments," *Zeitschrift der Savigny-Stiftung für Rechtsgeschichte, Kan. Abt. 102,* (1985): 147-214; Martin Brecht, "Luther und die Wittenberger Reformation während der Wartburgzeit," in *Martin Luther. Leben-Werk-Wirkung,* ed. Günter Vogler et al. (Berlin, 1983), 73-90.

Prague *Manifesto*. A few years later the Peasants' War, which Karl Marx called the "most radical fact of German history,"[17] showed in its totality the most radical expression of the reform movement. But even there "moderates" and "radicals" fought side by side, with the "moderates" being quite radical in relation to the immediately preceding period.

Hence, radicalism in the Reformation requires a relativistic and differentiated definition based on the state of the broader societal movement. But this is not enough. Relativization and differentiation are also needed for the criteria against which radicality can be measured: the social and political location of the different social forces that carried the movement of Reformation; the objectives they pursued; the theological-ideological arguments (including the relationship to the theological tradition); their relationship to the authorities; the instruments used by them to accomplish their goals; the consequences that clearly often deviated from the subjective goals. To put it more simply: it was possible that in one and the same "radical," and among various "radicals," considerable differences emerged in their degree of radicality, dependent on whether it was the break with theological tradition or the relationship with the secular authorities, implementing the Reformation "from above" or "from below," or the attitude towards the use of force, and other matters.

It should also be noted that, with the exception of Müntzer's views, more radical views concerning the right to resist tyrannical authorities existed prior to the Reformation. Joß Fritz and his *Bundschuh* programs of 1502 reflected views voiced almost three decades earlier.[18] At Taubertal in 1476 Hans Böheim invoked the divine right and demanded the abolition of all authority, including emperors, princes, and rulers. About the same time Wessel Gansfort published *De potestate ecclesiastica*, a pamphlet in which he developed his view of a voluntary social contract between subjects and authorities. Based on this natural law he called upon vassals to resist clerical and secular authorities, removing them if they violated the contract. Gansfort insisted "that emperor, king, prince and master . . . should be refused obedience if they do malice, one is obliged to drive the government away."[19] The views of these men regarding authority and the right to resistance reflected a degree of radicalism seldom seen in the so-called radicals of the Reformation. However, this radicality became societally effective only to a limited degree, or remained ineffective until the time when Luther, very much subservient to the political authorities and from the very beginning extremely moderate in his relationship with secular authorities, prepared the ground for Müntzer and the peasants.

---

[17]Karl Marx, "Einleitung zur Kritik der Hegelschen Rechtsphilosophie," in *Werke*, 1:386.

[18]See in summary form Laube et al., *Illustrierte Geschichte*, 53ff., 58ff., 96ff., 101ff.

[19]Citation according to a German translation of the pamphlet of 1530, in the forthcoming *Vom Bauernkrieg zum Täuferreich*. The Latin original is in: *Opera M. Wesseli Gansfortii Groningensis*, (Groningen, 1614), 748-71.

This applies in a similar way to other criteria. Let us take, for example, the willingness to use force as a decisive criterion of radicality. Here Sickingen's Knights' Rebellion would have to be included in the Radical Reformation. Sickingen and his knights, ideologically supported by humanists and reformers such as Hutten, Kettenbach, Oecolampadius, Bucer, Aquila, Cronberg, and Schwebel, saw their war against the Elector and Archbishop of Trier as their contribution to the Reformation, in the interest of the adoption of evangelical truth.[20] By contrast, the pacifist groupings among the Anabaptists should not at all be counted among the Radical Reformation. There also was no congruence between the Radical Reformation and the Reformation "from below," or the moderate Reformation and the Reformation "from above." In many towns the Magisterial Reformation was brought about—or accompanied—by a popular movement "from below." Conversely, there were radical varieties of the Reformation which enjoyed the support of the magistracy, for example in Müntzer and Pfeiffer, in Waldshut with Hubmaier, in Nikolsburg with Hubmaier and temporarily with Hut, and in Münster.

Specific isolated criteria are themselves not sufficient to label a person or an event of the Reformation as "radical." One must state explicitly which particular facet is meant. The problem is to find a common denominator, to bundle the criteria and to apply them in all their complexity. In the final analysis a yardstick is required which, irrespective of all relativizations and individual aspects, makes it possible to determine the radical facets in a revolution and accompanying it. For the denominational church historian this yardstick is, as a rule, his belief. Scholars of the Reformation and Anabaptism have long operated on the basis of their belief of free church movements and their polemics against others. But the historian who is intent on portraying societal totality—and here I include the non-Marxist social-historical research of the Reformation period—needs a different yardstick. That yardstick can only be the reference to a "society-wide context," as formulated by Goertz. "Radical would thus be any idea and any action that attacks the societal foundations, even if they had aims that were quite different from societal aims."[21] The Marxist historian will go a step further by determining, on the basis of the theory of formation, the social content of the existing order as the transition from feudalism to capitalism and by measuring the degree of social engagement against the historical needs and possibilities in this process of transition. The central category for this is the notion of social progress. I mention this only in passing, without further elaboration. In any case, the criterion for

[20]M. Meyer, "Sickingen, Hutten and die reichsritterschaftlichen Bewegungen in der deutschen frühen Revolution," *Jahrbuch für Geschichte des Feudalismus* 7 (1983); Martin Brecht, "Die deutsche Ritterschaft und die Reformation," *Ebernburg-Hefte* 3 (1969); Volker Press, "Ein Ritter zwischen Rebellion und Reformation. Franz von Sickingen (1481-1523)," *Blätter für pfälz. Kirchengeschichte* 50 (1983).

[21]Goertz, *Radikale Reformatoren*, 17.

radicality is what the historian, after analyzing all social conditions, social forces, possibilities, etc., concludes to have been implementable and this in the sense of the definition of the Reformation discussed above.

Viewed from a societal content it is possible to identify two essentially different radical groups or currents of the Reformation between 1522 and 1525: the bourgeois-radical group and the "People's Reformation" movement, to use a loose and as yet undefined term. The bourgeois-radical group encompassed all those whose (albeit quite different) views, efforts, and actions aimed to implement Reformation in a consistent, speedy fashion without hesitating, without moving beyond the framework of the existing or incipient bourgeois society and with a general orientation toward the ideals of the upper and lower middle classes of the towns. Their theological ideas were sometimes different from Luther. For example, in the question of the sacraments and in the iconoclastic controversy, they were more intensely influenced by mystical views, as it is expressed above all in the category *gelassenheit* (renunciation). Nevertheless, in terms of their social relevance their theology did not principally go beyond Luther.

In contrast to Luther, they addressed themselves more intensely to the "common man," especially to the lower and upper middle classes in towns and to the peasants (*Karsthans*), as the subjects and objects of the Reformation. Compared to Luther, they had a more critical attitude toward the secular authorities, without recognizing, however, any right of resistance or even use of force by the "common man" against the authorities. When controversies broke out in towns and in the countryside during the Peasants' War, they sided with the insurgent peasants and citizens, at least temporarily and inconsistently. They made great demands on the authorities based the principle of love, especially with regard to their exercise of authority vis-à-vis vassals. Their social-ethical views did not go far beyond those held by Luther in his *Open Letter to the Christian Nobility* and his pamphlets *Against Usury*, but they consistently tried to implement them in their communities with the help of the magistracies. By and large, this group has so far been insufficiently studied. Its prototype was Andreas Karlstadt[22] by his activities in Wittenberg and Orlamünde as well as his relations and influence on later Anabaptists and Spiritualists, like Melchior Hoffman, and Ludwig Hätzer. His actions in Rothenburg during the Peasants' War would certainly need further elucidation. Included in this group were Gerhard Westerburg and Jakob Strauß. Westerburg, a relative of Karlstadt, headed the insurgent movement of the lower and upper middle classes against the patrician council in Frankfurt during the Peasants' War and substantially influenced the forty-six Frankfurt Articles which included the demands of the rural countryside and gained an importance for the urban movement similar to the Twelve Articles for the

[22]See the essay of Siegrid Looß in this volume and the literature indicated there.

rural movement.[23] Jakob Strauß provoked the Eisenach usury dispute in 1523 because of his radical views on the question of interest and usury. His criticism of the authorities and his theology of the Cross prepared the ground for the Peasants' War, even though after his flight he defended himself against the charge of insurgency–as did Karlstadt–and distanced himself from the uprising.[24] The inclusion of Balthasar Hubmaier[25] in this group during his time in Waldshut must be considered. Within this group, undoubtedly, there were also the early writings of Ludwig Hätzer[26] and perhaps of Hans Denck, though the latter might be better grouped with Müntzer. Until 1522 Eberlin von Günzburg might have also been counted in this group. The transitions from this group to the popular reform group of Christoph Schappeler, Sebastian Lotzer, Johann Locher, and Clemens Ziegler appear to be fluid.[27] It would require more extensive studies to arrive at a demarcation between this group and the Zwinglian and South-German Reformation, or to explore the question of the points of contact between one or the other South-German reformers and the views of the radical-bourgeois Reformation.

The "People's Reformation" movement is principally distinct from the other currents of the Reformation. I use this term, introduced by Marxist literature, for lack of a better one, but I am aware that originally it did not describe what is intended, because other varieties of the Reformation were also borne by and oriented toward the people. In reality, it was the outermost left wing that also emerged in later bourgeois revolutions and aspired to overcome not only existing society, but also any kind of class society.

[23]Adolf Laube et al., *Flugschriften der Bauernkriegszeit*, 2d ed. (Berlin 1978, also Cologne/ Vienna, 1978), 22, 59ff, 572ff; see also Westerburg's later self-portrayal in the tract *Wie die Hochgelerten von Coelln Doctores in der Gottheit und Ketzermeister den Doctor Gerhart Westerburg des Fegfewrs halben als einen unglaubigen verurtheilt und verdampt haben* (Marburg: Franz Rhode, 1533).

[24]See Hermann Barge, *Jakob Strauß. Ein Kämpfer für das Evangelium in Tirol, Thüringen und Süddeutschland* (Leipzig, 1937); J. Rogge, *Der Beitrag des Predigers Jakob Strauß zur frühen Reformationsgeschichte* (Berlin, 1957); see also the pamphlets on usury in Adolf Laube et al., *Flugschriften der frühen Reformationsbewegung (1518-1524)* (Berlin/Vaduz, 1983), 2:1073ff.; Laube et al., *Flugschriften der Bauernkriegszeit*, 178ff, 589ff.; Jakob Strauß, *Auffrühen woren, Evangelischen Christen für zukomen...*, (Nürnberg: Friedrich Peypus, 1525); idem, *Christenlich und wolgegrundet antwurt. . . Auff das ungüttig schmachbüchlin Johannis Coclei von Wenndelsteyn betreffen die auffruer* ([Speyer, Jakob Schmidt], 1526).

[25]See Torsten Bergsten, *Balthasar Hubmaier. Seine Stellung zu Reformation und Täufertum 1521 bis 1528* (Kassel, 1961).

[26]See J. F. Gerhard Goeters, *Ludwig Hätzer (ca. 1500-1529). Spiritualist und Antitrinitarier. Eine Randfigur der frühen Täuferbewegung* (Gütersloh, 1957).

[27]See Martin Brecht, "Der theologische Hintergrund der Zwölf Artikel der Bauernschaft in Schwaben von 1525. Christoph Schappelers und Sebastian Lotzers Beitrag zum Bauernkrieg," *Zeitschrift für Kirchengeschichte* 85 (1974): 30-64; Gustav Bossert, *Sebastian Lotzer und seine Schriften* (Memmingen, 1906); Paul Kalkoff, "Die Prädikanten Rot-Locher, Eberlin und Kettenbach," *Archiv für Reformationsgeschichte* 25 (1928): 128-150; Walter Zöllner, "Johannes Locher–ein Kämpfer der Bauernkriegszeit," in *Der deutsche Bauernkrieg und Thomas Müntzer*, ed. Max Steinmetz et al. (Leipzig, 1976), 191-97; R. Peter, "Le maraicher Clément Ziegler: l'homme et son oeuvre," *Revue d'histoire et philosophie religieuses* 34 (1954): 255-82.

Thomas Müntzer was the prototype and the outstanding figure of this current of the Reformation. Proceeding from a revolutionarily interpreted apocalypticism and influenced by mystical-spiritualist views, he expected the immediate coming of God's Kingdom on earth, not in a passive way, but through the active revolutionary assistance of the "elect" as God's chosen people. These were predestined, by following Christ in Cross and suffering, by the repudiation of all worldly possessions and all human passions, to destroy and to overcome the worldly order, that is, the last false Christian realm on earth. Müntzer's intentions were not aimed at any reform of existing conditions, or the restitution of past conditions, but at complete revolution in order to bring about the immediate rule of God and the establishment of Christian freedom and equality on earth. The beginning of the "People's Reformation" in the towns and the Peasants' War acted as catalyst for the formation and radical development of this theology for appealing to ordinary people, as it activated the people as the carrier of the force of the sword and the driving power of revolutionary change.

The ideology and practice of the extreme left wing were in this manifestation the work of Müntzer. He was followed by Heinrich Pfeiffer and, with somewhat less impact, by Simon Haferitz.[28] To this group also belonged Hans Hut, Hans Römerr, and temporarily Melchior Rinck.[29] A strong influence on Hans Denck by Müntzer may also have been possible, as was shown by theological comparisons of texts.[30]

A question remains regarding the classification of the revolutionary programs which did not derive from theology, but from revolutionary practice. These programs attempted a radical change of the societal situation without a deeper-going theological-ideological explanation. The *Tyrolean Land Order* of Michael Gaismair, the *Letter of Articles* of the Schwarzwald peasants, or the Taubertal Program invoked the Word of God for the common benefit.[31]

[28]On Heinrich Pfeiffer (against previous views) see L. Rommel, "Heinrich Pfeiffer und Thomas Müntzer oder die Geschichte einer Legende," *Jahrbuch für Geschichte des Feudalismus* 11 (1987). On Simon Haferitz see Laube et al., *Flugschriften der Frühen Reformationsbewegung*, 1:316-51 and the literature indicated there.

[29]Gottfried Seebaß, "Müntzers Erbe. Werk, Leben und Theologie des Hans Hut," (Theol. Habil., Erlangen, 1972); Richard van Dülmen, "Müntzers Anhänger im oberdeutschen Täufertum," *Zeitschrift für bayerische Landesgeschichte* 39 (1976): 883-91; E. Geldbach, "Die Lehre des hessischen Täuferführers Melchior Rinck," *Jahrbuch der hessischen kirchengeschichtlichen Vereinigung* 21 (1970): 119-35; Zschäbitz, *Zur mitteldeutschen Wiedertäuferbewegung*, passim.

[30]Günther Goldbach, "Hans Denck und Thomas Müntzer—ein Vergleich ihrer wesentlichen theologischen Auffassungen," (Theological Dissertation, Hamburg, 1969) insisted on Denck's independence from Müntzer. See, however, the remarks by James M. Stayer et al., "From Monogenesis to Polygenesis: The Historical Discussion of Anabaptist Origins," *Mennonite Quarterly Review* 49 (1975): 106ff, and Georg Baring, "Hans Denck und Thomas Müntzer in Nürnberg 1524," *Archiv für Reformationsgeschichte* 50 (1959): 145-81; Werner O. Packull, *Mysticism and the Early South German-Austrian Anabaptist Movement 1525-1531* (Scottdale: Herald Press, 1977).

[31]See Laube et al., *Flugschriften der Bauernkriegszeit*, 109, 110ff., 139ff.

These reformers, intent on shaping society according to God's Word, conceived themselves as the enforcers of the Reformation and should be classified as a radical wing of the Reformation. Since they resorted to revolutionary means to eliminate worldly class rule "so that no difference shall exist among the people . . . and a full equality would be [reached] in the land"[32] they should be counted as the extreme left. Such inclusion, however, strips the "People's Reformation" of its Müntzer-related homogeneity.

This leads us to the general question of the classification of radical ideas, personalities, and programs that grew out of the reform movement, affirmed it, yet lacked an autonomous theological base. Many of those involved in the conflicts of the Reformation had their ideological roots in Humanism and had points of contact with radical-bourgeois tendencies. They included Ulrich von Hutten, the pronouncements of Hans Sachs, the so-called Heilbronn Program[33] of the Peasants' War and its underlying anonymous reform pamphlet *Deutscher Nation Notdurft* (*Needs of the German Nation*),[34] which might be viewed as "moderate," when measured against the criteria of the extreme left of the Peasants' War, but was downright radical in the light of the political program of the burgher class. According to the criteria noted above they would have to be counted among the bourgeois-radical groupings.

The category "radical" itself does not say anything about the content of reality and the potentials of success inherent in the current or ideology that is so characterized. As any ideology, radical ideology remains ineffective as long as it is not accepted by society or by certain social forces. If it is accepted, its social character is primarily revealed by those who accept it. Its persuasiveness is ultimately decided by the strength of its supportive societal forces, by the relative power against others—especially the ruling and established powers, and by the totality of social conditions. Under the given conditions the assessment of reality by the bourgeois-radical forces was, undoubtedly, more accurate than that of the extreme left. However, the latter were by no means mere utopians. On the one hand, they were carried by an actual social basis, as became apparent especially during the Peasants' War, and they expressed their yearning for a life free from exploitation in social equality. On the other hand, they were able to contribute objectively to implementing attainable aims to the extent that they established themselves as a social movement. Finally, it was possible for radical forces temporarily and locally to hold their own. After the suppression of the Peasants' War and the consolidation of feudal power, the societal situation changed substantially. The Peasants' War had resulted in a polarization of forces in great camps, which was now lost. Any statement in favor of the cause of the insurgents and the outlawed leaders—Müntzer,

---

[32]Ibid., 139.

[33]Ibid., 73ff.

[34]Laube et al., *Flugschriften der frühen Reformationsbewegung*, 2: 760ff.

Karlstadt, Strauss, and other "enthusiasts"—was not only severely persecuted by the authorities, but also could no longer count on the support and solidarity of large social groups. It was hardly possible for radical views to be converted into (illusionary) upheaval plans, as with Hans Römer's plan to capture Erfurt.[35] From now on radicality referred to an ideal potential and at best to the aim of a radical transformation of church and society. This potential was highly heterogeneous. Recent research on Anabaptism indicates that it was split into many more or less small groups.[36] Every individual was able—provided he had the charisma and the qualities of a leader—to find adherents to his views, inspirations, and visions, if he provided a solution to the existing social conditions. As a rule, however, this was done secretively and in small conventicles, unless local authorities sympathized with such views (as in Nikolsburg) or for the time being tolerated them (as in Strasbourg). Münster was and remained a heroic exception.

Early Anabaptism (including the Spiritualists)[37] began within the radical currents of the early Reformation and the Peasants' War. Only the defeat in the Peasants' War inspired some Anabaptists to find their way to Schleitheim, and to a radical separation from the world. Nevertheless, Müntzerian views survived in Hut, Römer and, to a certain extent, even in Denck.[38] It is difficult to measure the lasting influence of Müntzer on Grebel and his circle, Hubmaier, the Münsterites, and others. Calvin A. Pater, has shown how Karlstadt and the bourgeois-radical group of the early Reformation decisively influenced Anabaptism.[39] This indicates that Anabaptists and Spiritualists continued the bourgeois-radical and "People's Reformation" currents of the Reformation in the years after the Peasants' War, reshaping them in accordance with new social conditions and at the same time developing their own individual forms. The much disputed question of the theological roots in each individual case—medieval heresies, mysticism, Christian Humanism, Luther, Zwingli, Karlstadt or Müntzer—appears in this context to be secondary for the historian. The basis for all of them, at least for the first generation, was provided by the experience gained in the wake of the Reformation controversies and the Peasants' War and by the unsatisfactory solution of the basic prob-

[35]See Zschäbitz, *Zur mitteldeutschen Wiedertäuferbewegung*, 67ff.; Paul Wappler, *Die Täuferbewegung in Thüringen von 1526-1584* (Jena, 1913), 364ff.

[36]On this and the following see especially Clasen, *Anabaptism* and Goertz, *Radikale Reformatoren*; also Hans-Jürgen Goertz, ed., *Umstrittenes Täufertum 1525-1975* (Göttingen, 1977); Stayer et al., "From Monogenesis," 83-122; Stayer, *Anabaptists and the Sword*; idem, "Die Schweizer Brüder. Versuch einer historischen Definition," *Mennonitische Geschichtsblätter* 34 (1977): 7-34.

[37]Marxist research from the very beginning embraced this thesis. See, in addition to Zschäbitz, Gerhard Brendler, *Das Täuferreich von Münster 1534/35* (Berlin, 1966).

[38]Seebaß, *Müntzers Erbe*; see also Günther List, *Chiliastische Utopie und radikale Reformation* (Munich, 1973), 140ff; Packull, *Mysticism*.

[39]Calvin A. Pater, *Karlstadt as the Father of the Baptist Movement* (Toronto: University of Toronto Press, 1984).

lem, i.e. the fundamental transformation of ecclesiastical and societal conditions, a transformation that was believed to be absolutely necessary. This was the decisive stimulus and the common point of departure which sought to ascertain God's will and searched for theological undergirding, in the setting of societal conflict providing ideological legitimization.

Some of the current theological studies read as though the Anabaptists of the sixteenth century had at their disposal enormous libraries of biblical, patristic, canonical, heretical, humanist, and reform works and formed their opinions on the basis of thoughtful study. At best, such was possible for some of the leading theological thinkers. The majority of laymen and of half-educated persons undoubtedly acquired their views from life experiences and from social conflict, from the Bible, and from casual conversations with like-minded persons. All were the products of the Radical Reformation, even though their opinions were nourished by other sources. They were compelled to utilize and to rework—on the basis of their own experiences and persuasions—the theological opinions which best helped them to live as Christians according to their own view, which the completely corrupt church and the secular order did not permit. Starting from this theological point of view they were looking for a principal alternative, even against the Magisterial Reformation which was beginning to establish itself. All established powers, independent of their views of secular authority, felt them to be a threat and fought against them. For this reason the Anabaptists and Spiritualists must be considered the continuation of the Radical Reformation, although they exerted considerably less societal effect than during the early bourgeois revolution when they met with widest response and enjoyed great support. It remains the task of scholarship to identify the degree of radicality of the different groupings, such as that of the Sword Wielders and of the Pacifists or *Stäbler* in terms of their social impact.

"The time is not yet ripe for a comprehensive narrative of the 'Radical Reformation,'" wrote Goertz in 1978.[40] Although during the past eight years further attempts at elucidating the personalities and events of the "Radical Reformation" have led to considerable results, Goertz' assessment is still largely applicable. Radicalism remains a problem of research of the history of the early Reformation.

[40]Goertz, *Radikale Reformatoren*, 19.

The Peasants' War
Unidentified woodcut (ca. 1550s?)

Radicalism in the Early Reformation:
Varieties of Reformation in Church and Society

Hans J. Hillerbrand[1]

IT SURELY IS A WINSOME TRUISM—and thus a safe way to begin this paper—that the early years of the Reformation in Germany were an exceedingly diverse scene. Since they were dominated by the overtowering figure of Martin Luther, the vocal presence of other figures and the implications of that presence are not always fully acknowledged. In the years between 1518 and 1525 a diversity of thought and action was proposed under the general banner of reform and renewal. Hutten, Sickingen, Storch, or Eberlin are names that come to mind no less than Karlstadt, Bucer, or Oecolampadius. They all epitomize the diversity just noted. Sickingen and Hutten led the Knights' Rebellion which sought to take over ecclesiastical property; Nicholas Storch claimed, together with the two other Zwickau Prophets, Stübner and Drechsel, to possess the teaching of the Spirit, uttered dire apocalyptic warnings, and denounced infant baptism.

During those years, the *causa Lutheri* increasingly turned into a widespread and ubiquitous desire for renewal and reform. Political, economic, and social goals no less than religious and theological ones were advocated. Earlier reform proposals and grievances were echoed. It was a polyphonic choir, and not all sang out of the same hymnal.[2]

From the beginning Catholics had no problem at all with this diversity. Martin Luther and all who echoed him were heretics. Ironically, a similar categorical judgment was voiced by Luther who stridently denounced all who disagreed with him. They were *Schwärmer*, enthusiasts, a term which Gordon Rupp once transliterated as "too many bees chasing too few bonnets."[3] Other equally uncomplimentary epithets were employed with ease and nonchalance: rebellious spirit, Satan, heavenly prophets, murderous spirits.[4] Needless to say, those who were so included voiced objection to this indiscriminate view of things. Huldrych Zwingli, for one, refused to be equated with the Anabaptists and other dissenters, while the Anabaptists vigorously denied any kinship with Thomas Müntzer. Still, the notion that there was an essential unity of all Reformation "radicals," and that their thought was a far cry from what was

---

[1] This paper was intended as a parallel to the essay of Adolf Laube.

[2] The transmission of reform ideas through the printed page and the pulpit is extensively discussed in several of the essays in Hans-Joachim Köhler, ed., *Flugschriften als Massenmedium der Reformationszeit* (Stuttgart, 1981).

[3] George Rupp, "Luther and Zwingli," in *Luther Today* (Decorah, Iowa: Luther College Press, 1957), 147.

[4] For example WA 18, 72.

perceived to be the biblical splendor of the major reformers, has tended to carry the historiographical day, a few notable exceptions, such as Gottfried Arnold in the late seventeenth century, notwithstanding.[5]

In our own century, in the context of a lively Reformation scholarship, these dissenters have been the object of a great deal of scholarly attention even as much effort has been expended to delineate a comprehensive conceptualization of dissent in the Reformation, which Rufus H. Jones—in resignation or bewilderment—once called a veritable banyan tree. Roland H. Bainton introduced the concept of the 'Left Wing' of the Reformation and defined it as those "who separated church and state and rejected the civil arm in matters of religion."[6] Bainton argued that the Left Wing was also "more radical" with regard to church organization, sacraments, and creeds. This concept of the 'Left Wing' of the Reformation was very much in vogue in Reformation scholarship until George H. Williams proposed the term Radical Reformation.[7] While not the first instance of the scholarly use of the term, Williams was the catalyst to give it widespread acceptance. Its extensive use in recent years notwithstanding, there has prevailed considerable uncertainty about its precise definition. There is scholarly consensus about the need to view the "radicals" of the Reformation objectively and not with ecclesiastical bias, but there is continuing disagreement about the importance of Reformation dissent, its essence, and its cohesiveness.

*   *   *

The purpose of this paper is to reflect on the dynamics of the emergence of dissent in the early Reformation. Simply put, the paper seeks to address the question why there should have been a 'Radical Reformation' at all? Our focus is not so much the complex subtleties of the emergence of Reformation dissent, but the broader dynamics of the early Reformation that led to this emergence. At issue, in other words, is the broader framework of the early Reformation. What does it mean to speak of a 'Radical Reformation' or of 'radicalism' in the Reformation?

---

[5]Gottfried Arnold, *Unpartheyische Kirchen- und Ketzer Historien* (Frankfurt, 1699).

[6]Roland H. Bainton, "The Left Wing of the Reformation," *The Journal of Religion* 21 (1941): 124-34.

[7]George H. Williams, *The Radical Reformation (Philadelphia: Westminster, 1962), 846 ff. Williams first used the term 'Radical Reformation' in his 1957 Spiritual and Anabaptist Writers,* Library of Christian Classics No. 25 (Philadelphia: Westminster, 1957). He recently published a reevaluation: "The Radical Reformation Revisited," *Union Seminary Quarterly Review* 39 (1984): 1-24, in which he discusses the responses to the term 'Magisterial Reformation' as well as the term 'radical'. The Spanish language edition of his *Radical Reformation, La Reforma Radical* (Mexico City, 1983), includes an extensive reaction to the critics of Williams' concept of Radical Reformation.

Any discussion of the terms 'Radical Reformation' or 'radicalism' must acknowledge that these terms cannot be defined apart from the Reformation. And all nomenclature pertaining to the Reformation, in whole or in part, presupposes value judgments. The very term 'Reformation', denoting 'reform' (or a historical epoch denoting 'reform') has been highly objectionable to Catholics who have seen the Reformation as revolt or heresy, rather than as reform or, at any rate, not as legitimate reform in the medieval tradition. Only latter-day ecumenical liberality has obscured that for centuries Catholics spoke of the Protestant 'revolt' and rejected any understanding of the Reformation as authentic church reform.[8]

The term 'Reformation' may be said to have begun historically with a broad and general, and ended with a rather restricted and narrow definition. In the fifteenth century, it meant comprehensive reform of society; by the early seventeenth century, it referred to the renewal of church and theology as undertaken by the major reformers, Luther, Zwingli, Calvin. Part of the current debate about the meaning of the Reformation relates to the question of its definition, which in turn is linked to the assessment of the state of society in the early decades of the sixteenth century. The analysis of the advocacy of "reform" in the early sixteenth century takes on different meaning depending on how one assesses the state of society at the time. There is the 'powder keg' no less than the 'molasses' view of early sixteenth century German society—the one the notion of a world gone awry, beset by irreconcilable internal tensions, ready to explode any moment, the other the view of a society anxious, in transition, yet essentially stable.

There is also the matter of nomenclature. In recent years Reformation scholars have begun to realize that the term 'Reformation' is encumbered by the requirement of encompassing too many divergent facets. To use different terms for different facets of early sixteenth century events makes a great deal of sense. In particular, two terms—'reform' and 'reformation'—are useful, the former referring to efforts that were primarily concerned with social and political change, the latter foremostly with theology and church. Admittedly, this is an arbitrary, but helpful distinction which must be cognizant of the fluid lines connecting both phenomena.

The term 'Reformation', then, derived from the reformers' self-understanding, encompasses the range of ideas and events that relate to the delineation of new theologies different from, and the eventual establishment of churches independent of, Roman Catholicism. This Reformation had a concomitant dimension of societal change, with numerous expressions, depending on time and place. We must raise the question if this Reformation, so defined, was indeed the dramatically dominant German phenomenon

---

[8]The best survey still is E. W. Zeeden, *The Legacy of Luther* (Westminster, Md., 1954).

between 1517 and 1525. One may see in Germany during those years a broad movement of social change—reform—which had religious ramifications or see a movement of religious change—Reformation—with societal ramifications. Underlying these alternatives is the question of the inner core or momentum of change. The current notion, propounded with energy and emphasis by the new breed of social historians, of seeing the Reformation, in Robert Scribner's words, as a "social event, and to investigate it is to investigate the nature of social reality and of social processes," becomes problematic in terms of our definition.[9] To the point is Rainer Wohlfeil with his acknowledgement of the religious impetus of Martin Luther, which related to a universally disoriented society and its comprehensive renewal through the gospel.[10]

The *causa Lutheri*, with its religious point of departure, its concern for simple faith, its demand for Christian renewal, and its criticism of the church, let loose a wide range of responses, virtually all of which had been voiced before. Diversity and heterogeneity were the key elements in the early years of the Reformation.

In passing we may note that, if the term 'Reformation' is used for events in all European countries, our definition must be mindful of this European dimension. If the Reformation is defined as a movement for fundamental change in society, triggered by religion, events in England should conform to this definition. If not, a different term or a different definition is necessary. No matter how well the definition fits the German course of events, unless analogous events in other countries fit this definition, it should not be used. This common-sense stricture is not always honored, even though the term 'analogous', which calls for precise definition, allows for latitude. Most of the scholarly discussion of the conceptual issues focuses on Germany and leaves non-German events unconsidered.

The terms 'radical' or 'Radical Reformation', our standard nomenclature for Reformation 'dissent', are plagued, much like the term 'Reformation', by presuppositions and value judgments. George H. Williams, in proposing the term Radical Reformation, derived from the semantics of 'radical' the notion that the radicals consistently sought to return to the biblical roots. This definition in a way reiterated an analogous distinction between 'reformation' and 'restitution', the one expressing a concept of reform that focused on the church of the third or fourth century as norm, the other a concept of reform going back to the New Testament.[11] Such a distinction is problematic. After all, all

[9]Robert Scribner, "Is there a Social History of the Reformation?" *Social History* (1976): 505.

[10]Rainer Wohlfeil, *Einführung in die Geschichte der deutschen Reformation* (München, 1982), 72ff.

[11]The differentiation was introduced by Franklin H. Littell, "The Anabaptist Doctrine of the Restitution of the True Church," *Mennonite Quarterly Review* 24 (1950): 33-52. My comments above should make it clear that I disagree with this perspective. See my "Anabaptism and History," *Mennonite Quarterly Review* 45 (1971): 107ff, and the evaluation of the issue by John H. Yoder, "Anabaptism and History," in *Umstrittenes Täufertum*, ed. Hans-Jürgen Goertz (Göttingen, 1975), 244ff.

reformers meant to be faithful interpreters of the biblical message and sought to restore apostolic Christianity. Surely, Martin Luther can be said to have gone to the "roots" by his iteration of the Apostle Paul. The differences among the reformers were derived from the different ways they defined the "roots" of biblical Christianity. Thus, most reformers affirmed the doctrine of the Trinity as authentically biblical, whereas Michael Servetus and his followers saw it as post-biblical perversion. The use of theological criteria to establish the viability of a *Radical* Reformation thus gets bogged down in theological value judgments.

There is consensus that the meaning of 'radical' is always defined by circumstances at a given time. In other words, what is radical at one time may cease to be so a short time later. 'Radical' then refers to the categorical break with the immediate past, even regardless of substance or content of positions held. According to this definition Luther was radical in 1517-18 as was Zwingli a bit later. Ten years later they were still radical in relation to Catholic thought, but now there were reformers who had broken with them and, therefore, were radical, while Luther and Zwingli, in relationship to them, were not. We may label these dissenting reformers 'radical', even though they were theologically closer, in some respects, to Catholic thought than were either Luther or Zwingli.

Another option is to define as 'radical' reformers all those for whom reform meant a complete alteration of existing societal structures, if (the addition is important) this alteration was proposed with an explicit theological point of reference. Of course, given the linkage between church and society in the sixteenth century, any attempt at reform in church and theology entailed societal consequences: the course of events in every center of the Reformation illustrates this. Such consequences in society could, however, be seen in a limited or a comprehensive context–the introduction of an "order for the poor" or the repudiation of existing constitutional structures are illustrations that come to mind. Luther's *Open Letter to the Christian Nobility* expressed the former, Müntzer's tracts of 1524/25 the latter.[12] Only a fundamental attempt and pursuit of social change fits this definition of 'radical' reform.

I find the definition of the Radical Reformation attractive. Accordingly, I would define as radical reformers only those who undertook to alter the existing societal order on the basis of religion.[13] The precise wording is important: the key element is not the attempt to alter society without an explicit theological point of reference nor is it the mere opposition to the existing

[12]I take this to be the position of Günter Mühlpfordt, "Radikal: eine Kategorie in Anwendung auf Reform, Reformation und Revolution," *Reform - Reformation - Revolution*, ed. Siegfried Hoyer (Leipzig, 1980), 156ff.

[13]W. Klaassen, "Doperdom als revolutie: een voorbeeld van 'confessionalisme' in de doopsgezinde geschiedsschrijving," *Doopsgezinde Bijdragen* 7 (1981): 109-15, makes a similar point about the use of the term 'revolution' which he wants to be confined to efforts at societal transformation, for example, those of Michael Gaismair.

social order. The key element was the determination to change the societal order on religious grounds. That was rare. To be sure, our definition has the liability of reducing the bewildering pantheon of would-be radicals to very few. There is, in other words, not much of a 'radical' Reformation left. Thereby, we are bereft of a term that would sort out the pantheon of dissent, an assignment which George H. Williams ventured to carry out so valiantly. For this pantheon of manifestations of reform we best use purely descriptive terms—'Melchiorite,' 'Socinian,' 'Hutterite'; etc.

*   *   *

It has become commonplace in recent Reformation scholarship not to refer to the years before 1525 as 'Reformation' (reserving the term for the time of formal ecclesiastical changes that occurred afterwards) and instead to use the term 'evangelical movement' or 'movements' (the latter to denote the multiplicity of manifestations). This distinction characterizes the course of events which began sometime after 1517 as an evolutionary process which extended over almost a full decade before it reached that full fruition for which the term Reformation is properly in order. By the same token, caution would seem to be in order even when speaking about an evangelical 'movement' or 'movements' for those years, for these terms conjure up characteristics of cohesiveness, clarity of direction, and collective thought and action.[14] Such did not altogether characterize the situation of the early 1520s. There were, of course, local movements of reform even as the larger situation may be described in terms of the increasingly ubiquitous presence of such local movements. Still, it seems best to speak of a "wave" of reform as characteristic of the time between 1520 and 1524—or to be fully mindful of the relative lack of structure in the quest of reform. Franz Lau used the phrase *Wildwuchs der Reformation* (wild growth) which graphically evokes the notion of uncontrolled growth, development, and change.[15] Precisely that was the case.

If we inquire into the cause for such pursuit of reform, current scholarly vogue refers us the theme of anticlericalism during those years as the key for the widespread echo to Luther: people were tired of arrogant, ignorant, immoral priests, and resented them. But one must be cautious in this regard.[16]

---

[14]Robert Scribner, who speaks of a 'movement' in the half-decade before 1525, defines the term as involving "cohesiveness of thought and action." See his "The Reformation as a Social Movement," in: *Stadtbürgertum und Adel in der Reformation*, ed. W. J. Mommsen (Stuttgart, 1979), 54ff.

[15]Franz Lau, *Reformationsgeschichte bis 1532. Die Kirche in ihrer Geschichte III* (Göttingen, 1964), 17.

[16]The point is emphatically made in current literature. See H. J. Cohn, "Anticlericalism in the German Peasants' War," *Past and Present* 83 (1979): 3-31; Hans-Jürgen Goertz, "Aufstand gegen die Priester. Anticlericalismus und reformatorische Bewegung," in *Bauer, Reich und Reformation*, ed. Peter Blickle (Stuttgart, 1982), 182-209. A demurrer was voiced by Bernd Moeller, "Was wurde in der Frühzeit der Reformation in den deutschen Städten gepredigt?" *Archiv für Reformationsgeschichte* 75 (1984): 191.

The theme is not at all as strikingly prominent in the pamphlets of the time as some studies have suggested; the most popular tracts of Luther–the most popular writer–between 1519 and 1522 are devoid of it. Moreover, one must ponder the question if, in fact, a negative sentiment is capable to arouse widespread support.

The popular tracts of the time conveyed the positive message of deep and renewed spirituality. The message as one of essentials, of general exhortation (into which specific theological points could well be read), rather than of specific theological (Lutheran) affirmations.[17] Such general exhortations surely fit what people–illiterate and, after all, untrained in theology–could understand and, for that matter, wanted to understand. The topics of the tracts were prayer, death and dying, the use of the sacraments, etc. Of course, there was the presumption that things were not what they should be. Of course, there was criticism of the lukewarm spirituality and worldliness of the church. But the overriding tenor of the publications was positive, extolling the splendor of true Christian spirituality.

The common denominator was the invocation of the Word of God as ordering principle for individuals, the church, and society. Its focus was piety, its goal was what was called the liberation of imprisoned consciences.[18] Goals of social reform were verbalized and incompatible emphases and orientations stood side by side without clarification or resolution. Luther's *Letter to the Christian Nobility* dramatically contributed to the diversity since it seemed to advocate a comprehensive rather than narrow definition of reform.

A crucial change in the course of events occurred when the different emphases with respect to the meaning of reform turned into explicit disagreements. The first instance was, of course, the appearance of the Zwickau Prophets in Wittenberg and their insistence on immediate ecclesiastical change, direct revelation, and repudiation of infant baptism. Since the literary fall-out of that episode was modest, and Luther's heavy intrusion quickly calmed the waters, no broader consequences followed. Still, the disturbances were a harbinger of things to come–the conviction on the part of some that it was necessary to "complete" the task of reform and renewal. This was different from, say Ulrich von Hutten, whose differences with Luther or Zwingli never turned into explicit and public disagreement. Above all, explicit disagreement meant the advocacy of immediate structural and empirical change. The

---

[17]See Paul Russell, "'Your sons and daughters shall prophesy ...' Common People and the Future of the Reformation in the Pamphlet Literature of Southwestern Germany to 1525," *Archiv für Reformationsgeschichte* 74 (1983): 122-40. Russell has a full monograph on the topic: *Lay Theology in the Reformation. Popular Pamphleteers in Southwest Germany 1521-1525* (Cambridge: Cambridge University Press, 1985). A related study, by Franziska Konrad, *Reformation in der Bäuerlichen Gesellschaft zur Rezeption reformatorischer Theologie im Elsass* (Stuttgart, 1984), shows how general was the perception of the theological subtleties among the common people.

[18]There are provocative musings by Heiko A. Oberman, "Reformation: Epoche oder Episode," *Archiv für Reformationsgeschichte* 68 (1977), esp. 106-9.

dissenters stressed not so much different ideas as the need for action, which characterized, at once, those for whom change was eminently political or economic. What followed was in all instances among those focused on religion a non-separatist thrust. The goal was not so much to establish a new and separate church, but to bring the efforts at reform and renewal already under way to a meaningful completion. This clearly characterized the situation in Zürich, where the reform parties were, certainly until the end of 1523, in essential agreement, but where the issues of images and the evangelical communion service brought about a confrontation between Zwingli and his impatient disciples.[19] The dynamics of the situation prompted all reformers to be optimistic about the possibility of influencing the larger course of events.[20] Since things were in a state of flux, and no definitive decisions about the meaning of reform and renewal had been made, one could not think otherwise. The goal was reform and renewal. A church separate from Rome or, for that matter, separate from Wittenberg or Zürich, was unthinkable. After all, one's own position was utterly persuasive. Separation became a possibility only once the impossibility of realizing one's own notion of reform had become clear. A different social commonwealth seemed to be in the range of possibilities.

The eventual outcome of this development, namely actual separation, has enticed scholars to trace the beginnings of the new ecclesiastical bodies as far back into the early years of the Reformation as possible. One must be cautious. To be sure, at one point all reformers, without exception, had to face the stark reality that the larger course of events (which differed, of course, for each reformer) did not favor them and that, short of returning to the Catholic Church, the only viable option was that of separation. It seems safe to say, however, that prior to the mid-1520s all efforts at "reformation," including those involving the Mass and its replacement by a new communion service, were not viewed as final and definitive, but as tentative. The fiction of "eventual reunion" was far stronger in the Germany of 1525 than in the two Germanies of 1987.

The first major public disagreement in the ranks of the reformers occurred when Andreas Karlstadt hurled his theological pronouncements against

---

[19]There is considerable literature of the so-called "turning point" of the Zwinglian Reformation in Zürich. It was triggered by John H. Yoder's scholarly restatement of the dissenters' traditional notion of Zwingli's deviation from his original goals. See his "The Turning Point of the Zwinglian Reformation," *Mennonite Quarterly Review* 32 (1958): 128-40. The view was contested by Robert C. Walton, "Was there a Turning Point of the Zwinglian Reformation?," *Mennonite Quarterly Review* 42 (1968): 45-57.

[20]I believe this certainly to be the case with respect to the emergence of Anabaptism, where the view of James M. Stayer, "Die Anfänge des schweizerischen Täufertums," in *Umstrittenes Täufertum*, 41ff has been countered by Charles Nienkirchen, "Reviewing the Case for a Non-Separatist Ecclesiology in Early Swiss Anabaptism," *Mennonite Quarterly Review* 56 (1982), 227ff. Stayer responded to Nienkirchen with "The Separatist Church of the Majority," *Mennonite Quarterly Review* 57 (1983): 151-55.

Luther and undertook "radical" ecclesiastical reforms in Orlamünde. This was
to be followed by Thomas Müntzer's strident indictment of Luther's understanding of the Christian faith. Thus outright confrontation occurred. It
served to clarify the existing situation with all of its complexities and
prompted the respective positions increasingly to emerge with uncanny clarity. And before 1525 was over, there had surfaced in Switzerland and in South
Germany, paralleling the Peasants' War, new manifestations of religious
reform committed to the sharply delineated goals of believer's baptism and the
believer's church. Something else had harshly manifested itself as well –and
that was a form of reform, personified by Thomas Müntzer, whose goal was
the revolutionary change of political structures based on theological notions.
In one respect Müntzer was but one of several proponents of reform who
differed with Luther and Zwingli. Yet in another respect the divergence was
fundamental in that Müntzer pursued a comprehensive change of existing
societal structures.

Our analysis thus far has focused in the main on facets of ecclesiastical and
theological change and we must pause and reflect if a broader picture can be
painted. The question is, of course, if certain social and political developments,
related to the Reformation, had profoundly "radical" propensity, with the
definition of 'radical' being that of categorical discontinuity with the immediate past. The answer is, of course, in the affirmative, with the Knight's Rebellion of 1522 and the Peasants' War of 1524/25 as the events that immediately
come to mind. The latter, in particular, had in its foremost manifesto, the
Twelve Articles, a program which saw religious change as prerequisite for,
fundamental social reform. Plainly, the Twelve Articles answer the question
about reform with the unequivocal statement that all of society must be
changed–and that this had to be done on the basis of Scripture.

This was "radical," indeed "radical Reformation."

*   *   *

It is true enough that the initial disagreement among reformers was essentially over the strategy and the timing of reform.[21] The parties disagreed over
the timeless question of how reform is best accomplished and over the "right
time" of change. It is not for nothing that the title of Karlstadt's tract *Ob Man
Gemach Faren*, of 1522, which addressed the issue, had a verbatim counterpart
in Robert Browne's *A Treatise of Reformation without Tarrying for Any* of 1582.
Some reformers wanted to move impatiently and with dispatch. Those with

[21]This is pointedly argued by H. W. Meihuizen, "Gab es einen Consensus Mennoniticus vor
der Taufe von 1525?" *Menn. Gesch. Bl.* 24 (1967): 72-81. Kenneth Davis, "Anabaptist Research
Today," *Mennonite Quarterly Review* 53 (1979): 207ff argues that by late 1524 Manz and Grebel
were clearly separatist.

the greatest influence on the course of events, however, opted for gradual change. While the key element was that of timing, differences in this regard (in Wittenberg, Zürich, or other places) soon became differences in theological perspective or expressed such differences. Certainly, by 1523, the substantive differences among the sundry voices of reform were beginning to be real.

At that time the "wave" of reform in Germany had reached a critical juncture. On a broad scale there occurred reflection and inventory taking. The enthusiasm personified by Martin Luther was beginning to run its course. To be sure, people had been challenged, changes were being considered but nowhere near the extent that had been hoped. A diversity of non-religious motives had seeped in from the beginning. "They use Luther only as a subterfuge," wrote Sebastian Lotzer, and Hans Sachs echoed, "You look to Luther to find a cloak for your own inappropriate behavior."[22] The authentic meaning of reform continued to be clouded.

The pamphlets of that time expressed this mood of reflection and took inventory of the state of affairs—the uncertainty of the meaning of reform; the incipient Catholic and governmental reaction against any reform impulses; the abortive uprising of the German knights; the pressing social questions, such as the tithe; the restlessness among the peasants. The time was that of a transition to a new stage of events.[23]

The point of departure for the emergence of Reformation "dissent" occurred when, prompted by such reflection, some reformers pitted their diverging perspective explicitly against that of their fellow reformers, notably, of course, against that of Luther and Zwingli, or drew consequences and formulated alternatives. Thereby, what had been a juxtaposition of views, an uneasy coexistence, an openness toward the future, became a tension. Diversity turned into opposition.

One can state the matter yet another way. The split in the movement of reform was the obvious outgrowth of different conceptions of the meaning of reform. On the face of things there were two lines of demarcation: that which pertained to the meaning of religious and theological reform and that which related to the matter of the comprehensiveness of reform. We can consider the differences between Karlstadt and Luther as representative of the former, the differences between Müntzer and Luther as representative of the latter.

No norm or standard must be read into this emergence of disagreement, even as 'dissent' is viable only as a descriptive term, simply denoting disagreement with a position previously enunciated. The desirability of caution in using the term becomes evident when we realize that to label Karlstadt a 'dissenter' might not cause misgivings; so to label Zwingli will. Of course, this

---

[22]Cited by Russell, "Common People," 131.
[23]This is the thrust of Russell's analysis, ibid., 139f.

is precisely how Luther labeled Zwingli, and given the fact that he offered a theological value judgment his stance is understandable.

It is easy to chide Martin Luther for his unwillingness to accept a peaceful coexistence with Orlamünde or Allstedt, or chide Zwingli for his unwillingness to accept dissent in his own ranks. The fact of the matter is, however, that all proponents of reform (Karlstadt's intermittent fickleness notwithstanding) were every bit as adamant and strident as they were. The difference was that some reformers were able to bring the full weight of their theological and political influence to bear on the situation. And that determined the actual course of events. Surely, not all of the clash was attributable to temperament or personality, a view which Gordon Rupp seemed to favor in his assessment of Müntzer. But we deprive ourselves of authentic insight into the complexity of the situation if we fail to acknowledge that temperament did play a critical role in that temperament does relate to strategy. And there was something else. The denunciation of the opponent, propounded with increasing shrillness, was precipitated not only by biblical understanding but also by the awareness that to acknowledge the possibility of diverse interpretations of Scripture meant confusion—and the inevitability of having to acknowledge once again the wisdom of the Catholic insistence on the need for the external authority of church or pope.

The "crisis" of 1523-25 and the concomitant reflections on the meaning of reform led to division in the ranks of the reformers. Historians from the German Democratic Republic have suggested that at this time the movement of reform spawned, at this time alongside its major Lutheran wing, two new major manifestations, namely a *bürgerlich-radikale Reformation* and *volksreformatorische Bewegung*.[24] The *bürgerlich-radikale Reformation*, represented by such men such as Karlstadt, Westerburg, and Strauss, sought a consistent realization of Luther's original religious and theological goals. The *volksreformatorische Bewegung*, in turn, was led by Thomas Müntzer, culminated in the uprising of the "common man," the Peasants' War, and wanted to change society.

On the face of things, this view seems plausible. As the general course of reform began demonstrably to slacken because of a lack of clear focus, new impulses appeared and sought to determine the agenda of reform. Still, the weakness of these two labels is that they are derived from class categories (*bürgerlich* and *volks*) and that they conjure up, once again, notions of cohesiveness and structure which, in my judgment, did not characterize the situation in the early 1520s. The authentic sense of the time was that the lines between the several reformers and their ideas were as fluid as the hues in a watercolor

[24]The earliest statement of this differentiation is in Max Steinmetz, "Die frühbürgerliche Revolution in Deutschland," in *Reformation oder frühbürgerliche Revolution?* ed. Rainer Wohlfeil (München, 1972), 51.

and as complex as a street map of Tokyo. We do best, therefore, not to systema-
tize the strands of reform.

*   *   *

In this context Anabaptism had its beginning in 1524/25. It proved to be
the major manifestation of dissent in the Reformation, albeit–and this is
important– only a "minor episode" in the larger history of the Reformation.[25]
James M. Stayer and his revisionist colleagues have vigorously reminded us in
recent years that we must see this beginning as "polygenesis" throughout
South Germany and Switzerland as well as the North rather than as
"monogenesis" in Zürich. The early Anabaptist movements–the plural is
important–were therefore reflective of diverse streams and a far cry from the
structured clarity of the Schleitheim Articles of 1527 which represent not so
much a restatement of existing normative Anabaptist views as the delineation
of a new position.

This view of Anabaptist origins places, as regards the Swiss situation, great
emphasis on the diversity of the time before January 1525 (the open break of
the Grebel group with Zwingli) and transfers the uncertainties of that time
into the period thereafter, so that Balthasar Hubmaier and Hans Hut become
major Anabaptist representatives of streams different from that of the Grebel
group. While details of this argument remain yet to be fully analyzed, the key
point for the purposes of our paper is clear and warrants endorsement: the rise
of Anabaptism was an expression of the "crisis" of 1523/24.

The opposition against tithes in Zürich and environs, the repudiation of
images, the quest for a new communion service, in short, the strategy to turn
the Reformation in Zürich into a different direction, was part and parcel of a
groping for direction and clarification. In Zollikon and Hallau, according to
admittedly evasive sources, there may have been a widespread popular movement, rallying around the issue of the tithe and the selection of the clergy by
the congregation, two standard themes in the story of the Reformation.[26]

There is no doubt but that the incipient Anabaptist conventicles did see
themselves as bringing Luther's and Zwingli's work of reform to consistent
completion, indeed, this sentiment proved to be the characteristic sentiment
for years to come. Luther, wrote the Hutterite *Chronicle*, broke the pope's
pitcher but kept the pieces in his hands.[27] The notions of the incompleteness
and inconsistency of the dominant manifestations of reform–Zürich and

---

[25]Claus-Peter Clasen, *Anabaptism. A Social History 1525-1618* (Ithaca: Cornell University Press, 1972).

[26]Stayer, "Die Anfänge des schweizerischen Täufertums," 47.

[27]A. J. F. Zieglschmid, ed., *Die älteste Chronik der Hutterischen Brüder* (Ithaca: Cornell University Press, 1943), 43.

Wittenberg—found a telling expression. Theologically the issue is somewhat complicated since some Anabaptists in their attempt to take Luther's thought to its consistent conclusion recurred to traditional theological notions.[28] In terms of the inner dynamics of the situation, however, this is a moot point: the Anabaptists demonstrably understood themselves as those who were completing the work of reform. They yearned for completeness. This is an important consideration, for it denotes that self-perception and perception by others are not necessarily identical.

We have touched on the incipient phase of Anabaptism for the reason of relating the origins of the movement to the broader course of the movement of reform between 1517 and 1525. The parallels between that broader course of events and the rise of Anabaptism are striking—the juxtaposition of diverse strands and objectives, the period of uncertainty, the process of clarification. However, the stories both of the larger Reformation and of Anabaptism entice us to see diversity or uncertainty as essence, or, for that matter, to view as equal in importance what, in fact, was not.[29]

*   *   *

We must ask about the essential points of divergence between the several streams of reform at the point in time when the Reformation divided. Needless to say, all reformers underwent change, felt differently about issues at different times and, in fact, did not always pursue consistent goals and objectives. Zwingli abandoned his earlier pacifism and Luther developed his views on baptism from 1520 onward. Konrad Grebel's letter to Müntzer expressed that early side of Luther quite clearly.[30] Indeed, the rise of Anabaptism is very much a case in point, for here we have a movement that modified a quest for general reform to one of separation, that did not start out as a sect, but ended as one.

First among the disagreements was the issue of the timing of reform. Those who counselled patience faced those who pressed for immediate action. Clearly, a host of considerations underlay the two respective positions—how pivotal was the issue in question? What was politically feasible? The fact remains, all the same, that two basically divergent dispositions sought to influence the course of events. The one faction accused the other of cowardice,

---

[28]This is the general argument of W. Klaassen, *Anabaptism: Neither Catholic nor Protestant* (Waterloo, 1973) and Kenneth Davis, *Anabaptism and Asceticism. A Study in Intellectual Origins* (Scottdale: Herald Press, 1974).

[29]I concur with the sentiment of Heinold Fast and Kenneth Davis that there was a normative Anabaptism and I would locate it in the stream that was "successful" and offered a distinct spirituality of its own. This notion does not speak, however, to the issue of the complexity of the early years. See Stayer, "Die Anfänge des schweizerischen Täufertums," 22.

[30]Martin Brecht, "Herkunft und Eigenart der Taufanschauung der Züricher Täufer," *Archiv für Reformationsgeschichte* 64 (1973): 147ff.

opportunism, and weakness, in short, of betraying the Gospel.[31] The key slogan was that of the *Schonung der Schwachen*.[32]

Historians have used the Miltonian phrase of "reform of the Reformation." It is not an altogether useful term for it presupposes that the Reformation was clearly delineated, already in place, and needed correction.[33] A better phrase might be the "completion" of the Reformation, in other words, the notion that some reformers wanted reform to continue and, thereby, go beyond the status quo. As far as these reformers were concerned, the quest for reform had become "stuck" and needed completion.

A second point of divergence had to do with the place of the political authorities in the process of reform. It was the contention of both Roland H. Bainton and George H. Williams (who introduced the term 'Magisterial Reformation') that the "radicals" were those among the reformers who disavowed the role of governmental authority in the pursuit of reform. Recent scholarship has pointed out that there was by no means unanimity among the radicals on this point, and that at least some were quite willing to enlist the support of government for the attainment of their brand of reform. The point is made not only for Balthasar Hubmaier but for others as well, notably for the Münster Anabaptists in the 1530s. But, no matter, for the fact is that all "radicals" had to come to grips with the reality at one point that they could only prevail in the face of opposition to governmental authority. They declared themselves prepared to do so—and marshaled biblical and theological support for their position.

Third, there was disagreement over the scope of reform. The question was simply if reform and renewal were to be confined to the ecclesiastical realm and focus on theology and church life, or if comprehensive societal reform was the crucial issue, or at any rate, the inevitable by-product of a new understanding of the Christian faith? This was the key element almost from the beginning of the controversy, with long uncertainty about the answer. Luther at first seemed to embrace a broad definition, note his tracts to the Christian nobility, but by 1524 he had gone on record that reform, should only focus on religion. Zwingli's *Sixty-seven Conclusions* did concede the hope for a different commonwealth. James Stayer and Hans-Jürgen Goertz have argued that in the beginning the Anabaptist movement epitomized such a comprehensive approach to reform: the social and political factors in the rise of early Swiss Anabaptism were important and, far from being committed to a policy of

---

[31]James M. Stayer, "Die Anfänge des schweizerischen Täufertums," 22.

[32]L. von Muralt und W. Schmid, eds., *Quellen zur Geschichte der Täufer in der Schweiz*, Vol. 1: *Zürich* (Zürich, 1952), 16.

[33]J. A. Oosterbaan, "The Reformation of the Reformation: Fundamentals of Anabaptist Theology," *Mennonite Quarterly Review* 51 (1977): 178ff.

withdrawal, the first Swiss Anabaptists strove for a "territorial base."[34] In Zürich the initial confrontation over strategy of reform focused on the need to reform the political or social structures of society. Such incipient sentiment quickly gave way—certainly in its major manifestation—to a strand of Anabaptism which had nothing to say about the political and social order, other than to stay aloof from it.

Third, there was disagreement over how to understand the essential Christian experience. The question was simple and basic: what did it mean to be a Christian? Through the centuries that question had been answered in various ways, even as it was Martin Luther's provocative answer which precipitated the Reformation controversy. The quest for Christian renewal entailed the questions of authentic Christian experience. In the early 1520s a "conversionist" and a "non-conversionist" stream began to face each other, those who argued that the Christian faith was inextricably linked to the experience of conversion, to the experience of a new life, and those who argued that the Christian life was one of repentance and sin.

This difference meant, of course, something very obvious, namely dissonance in theological perspective. While disagreement over the nature of Christian experience allows practically for only two answers, theological disagreement can call forth a seemingly endless variation. In Zürich the confrontation over the strategy of change turned into a divergence over the nature of the Christian experience and then into theological disagreement over baptism.[35] The ultimate issue was thus theological.

Related was a differing interpretation of the history of the Christian Church. There were opposing perspectives on what was variously called the "fall" of the true church, the "Babylonian Captivity" of the church, or even the disappearance of the true faith.

*   *   *

Finally, we must ask about the points of agreement among the reformers. On what issues did all reformers of the early years of the Reformation agree? The specifics are worth enumerating.

First, of course, was a set of common oppositions. There was a common enemy, a common critique. It was preeminently directed against the Catholic Church, the "Babylonian harlot." The charges were basic and categorical. The Roman Catholic Church no longer met biblical standards. It had become embroiled in worldly endeavors. The priests were ignorant, worldly, immoral, and illiterate. The pope was the Antichrist. All while various reformers had

[34]James M. Stayer, "The Swiss Brethren," *Church History* 47 (1978): 189.
[35]Muralt und Schmid, *Quellen zur Geschichte der Täufer in der Schweiz*, Vol. 1: *Zürich*, 23.

distinctive ways of expressing the sentiment, they all were in essential agreement.

Second, all reformers were visionaries in the sense of invoking an ideal, a golden age, a vision of a New Jerusalem. To be sure, they differed hopelessly when it came to describing this vision, but still, describe it they did. And their exuberant descriptions certainly were the reason why the Catholic polemicists were destined to be so wooden and cumbersome in their response. Catholics simply could not veer too far from the status quo, accept it, defend it; they were forced into the defensive by responding to the visions of lofty splendor of what was not, yet would be. It was not until much later in the Reformation that the reformers, too, had to address the issue of their status quo and acknowledge that the New Jerusalem perpetually glimmers ahead.

Third, all reformers redefined the traditional locus of authority. Most of them posited the authority of the Word as the new principle. As time passed, there surfaced a wide variety of definitions as to how that "Word" was to be interpreted. This was not an easy issue, and the problem of "word and spirit" hovers over these years. But, whatever the precise new locus, the old one which focused on the church was repudiated.

*   *   *

The early Reformation in Germany was a diverse phenomenon in which, in the early years, converged a number of unrelated or tenuously related objectives and goals. To affirm this heterogeneity is not to suggest that all manifestations were created equal or influential. Religious concerns were more prominent than non-religious ones, and some religious concerns were more prominent than others. It is a misreading of the dynamics of those years to suggest that any of the sundry impulses might have come to fruition; to do so ignores, at least in my judgment, the crucial importance of the charismatic leader in the course of events. Some of the reformers—notably Luther and Zwingli—possessed such qualities and events were bound to be significantly influenced by them.

When, by 1523, the diversity and inconclusiveness of the reform impulses became increasingly evident, a crystalization occurred. A crisis set in and a new stage of the development began. The house divided. Separate factions, increasingly distinct and recognizable, emerged, each motivated by a different notion as to the ideal society and the authentic Christian faith.

The use of the term 'radical' or 'Radical Reformation' in conjunction with the Reformation is possible in any number of definitions, as indeed Reformation scholars over the last two generations have given ample evidence of a deep need to do so. It seems fair to say, all the same, that none of the definitions has succeeded in silencing all demurrers or in removing endless qualifications. This is perplexing enough if we confine ourselves to the beginning of dissent (the years to 1525); the problem becomes virtually insoluble once we encompass the entire first half-century of the Reformation.

We return, in conclusion, to our opening question: Why should there have been a 'Radical' Reformation at all? The answer, so I should like to think, is clear. There was a 'Radical Reformation' simply because the Reformation movement itself was not focused. It was a general yearning for change and a desire for renewal. Certain expressions became dominant. The "dissenters" of the Reformation were those who proposed what we might call an "alternate" Reformation, that is, another way of defining both goal and strategy of reform. The term 'alternate Reformation' is much preferable to 'radical', despite an element of clumsiness, since it begs no questions of value or theological norms. The "radicals" proposed an alternate understanding of the meaning of the Christian faith and an alternate model of society. Their understanding of the faith was neither more comprehensive nor more radical than that of the "mainstream" reformers; it was different. At least that is how much the historian may say, based on the historian's methodology; theologians may present their ecclesiastical credentials and say more. By the same token, the category "radical" should be reserved for those instances where the exercise of religious conviction entailed an explicit attack upon the existing societal order.

Andreas Bodenstein von Karlstadt.
Unique likeness in Basel University Museum.

Radical Views of the Early
Andreas Karlstadt (1520-1525)

Sigrid Looß

SINCE THE GREAT CONTROVERSY between Hermann Barge and Karl Müller at the beginning of this century[1] about the work and writings of Andreas Bodenstein, called Karlstadt, there have been repeated attempts to explore specific aspects of Karlstadt's reform efforts, mostly in relation to the Lutheran Reformation.[2] In this setting Karlstadt was at times viewed in a confessional way which has only changed since the late 1950s.[3] The recent publications of Ronald Sider and Ulrich Bubenheimer are basic studies of Karlstadt's life and thought.[4] The question of the nature of the controversy between Luther and Karlstadt in 1521/22 which had been raised by James Preuss[5] and Ronald Sider was recently addressed again by Martin Brecht and Ulrich Bubenheimer.[6] But even more recent research has not been able to answer fully the question of why Luther and his followers disapproved of Karlstadt so categorically. There seem to be no serious differences in basic theological orientation, even though as early as 1520 Karlstadt began to develop different nuances and emphases regarding sanctification, penance, and particularly the sacraments. What should no longer be considered viable—since we know that Karlstadt was three years younger than Luther—is a psychological explanation

---

[1]Hermann Barge, *Andreas Bodenstein von Karlstadt* (Leipzig, 1905); Karl Müller, *Luther und Karlstadt* (Tübingen, 1907).

[2]See among others Martin Wähler, *Die Einführung der Reformation in Orlamünde* (Erfurt, 1918); Erich Hertzsch, *Karlstadt und seine Bedeutung für das Luthertum* (Gotha, 1932).

[3]Gordon Rupp, "Andrew Karlstadt and the Reformation Puritanism," *Journal of Theological Studies* n.s. 10 (1959): 308-26; Hans J. Hillerbrand, "Andreas Bodenstein of Carlstadt," *Church History* 35 (1966): 379-98; Friedel Kriechbaum, *Grundzüge der Theologie Karlstadts* (Hamburg, 1967).

[4]Ronald J. Sider, *Andreas Bodenstein von Karlstadt, The Development of His Thought 1517-1525* (Leyden, 1974); Ulrich Bubenheimer, *Consonantia Theologica et Iurisprudentiae. Andreas Bodenstein von Karlstadt als Theologe und Jurist zwischen Scholastik und Reformation* (Tübingen, 1977).

[5]James S. Preuss, *Carlstadt's "Ordinaciones" and Luther's "Liberty": A Study of the Wittenberg Movements 1521-1522*, Harvard Theological Studies 27 (Cambridge: Harvard University Press, 1974).

[6]Martin Brecht, "Luther und Karlstadt. Der Beginn des Abendmahlsstreites 1524/25 und seine Bedeutung für Luthers Theologie," *Zeitschrift der Savigny Stiftung für Rechtsgeschichte, Kan. Abt.* 70 (1984): 196-216.; Ulrich Bubenheimer, "Scandalum et ius divinum. Theologische und rechtstheologische Probleme der ersten reformatorischen Innovationen in Wittenberg in 1521/22," ibid. 59 (1973): 263-342; idem, "Luthers Stellung zum Aufrühen Wurzeln des landesherrlichen Kirchenregiments," ibid. 71 (1985): 147-214. Carter Lindberg, too, touches on the issue in his study: "The Conception of the Eucharist According to Erasmus and Karlstadt," in *Les dissidents du XVIᵉ siècle entre l'humanisme et le catholicisme* (Baden-Baden, 1983), 79-94.

of the disagreement as a dispute of rivals, the older Karlstadt and the younger Luther.[7] The variation offered by Preuss and Sider[8] who attribute the conflict between the two Wittenberg reformers to different notions of strategy and tactics of practical church reform, in other words, in the final analysis to political-ecclesiastical disagreements, is a more objective approach, especially in view of Karlstadt's efforts at Reformation. In the volume *Radical Reformers* Sider placed Karlstadt "between liberalism and radicalism," and thereby greatly relativized Karlstadt's position. This agreed with the tenor of Hans-Jürgen Goertz' preface to the volume which stressed the fluid lines among the so-called radical reformers and emphasized the impossibility of establishing common criteria for specific radical types and currents.

Indeed, the term "radical," when applied to historical processes, activities, and modes of thinking, must always be related to a specific time and particular phase of societal events. The progress of the historical process means that the category "radical" becomes relative. It simply expresses a tendency which denotes the degree of tension between the existing norm and an actual or imagined goal. According to the Marxist understanding of the epoch of the Reformation and the Peasants' War, which is seen as having a revolutionary character, this tension was subject to rapid change and related to all spheres of society and all ways of thinking. In line with the intellectual and social conditions of the sixteenth century such thinking was theologically oriented. Action within the movement of reform was ultimately aimed at restraining the political power of the old church in favor of the bourgeois and secular and noble classes. The Reformation was part and parcel of a revolution, whose character is the outgrowth of the beginning of the epoch of which it was part. At the end of the fifteenth century processes set in which marked the transition from feudalism to capitalism. Early modes of bourgeois thinking were being formed and action was being interpreted which helped promote the development of the bourgeoisie as a class in the modern definition. This is the overriding perspective under which I view the modes of thought and the courses of action in the time between 1517 and 1525/26. Thus the application of the term "radical" to modes of thought and action during the Reformation is related to a societal process.[9] It expresses social change in society or the perception of such change.

---

[7]Ulrich Bubenheimer discovered a commemorative paper published on the occasion of Karlstadt's death in Basel: Einblattdruck, UB Bern, Hospinian 7.

[8]The opinions of the two are again pronounced in Sider's study of Karlstadt, in *Radikale Reformatoren. 21 biographische Skizzen von Thomas Müntzer bis Paracelsus*, ed. Hans-Jürgen Goertz (München, 1978), 25.

[9]See the paper by Adolf Laube in this volume as well as his essay "Die Reformation als soziale Bewegung," *Zeitschrift für Geschichtswissenschaft* 33 (1985): 424-41.

The characterization of the early Karlstadt as "radical" presupposes an answer to the following questions: From which valid norms of the social process did his ideas and actions dissent? To what extent did his thought and action cause, directly or indirectly, social change? To what degree did he accept existing conditions? To what degree did he reject them? Was he the representative of the interests of a specific social class?

It must also be noted at the outset that ever since historians of the German Democratic Republic have discussed the issues of the early bourgeois revolution, this phenomenon has not been seen as politically and socially homogeneous. Different stages with socially different groups of representatives have been taken for granted, even as they characterize the degree of radicalization until the time of the Peasants' War. Gerhard Brendler has noted "that the German early bourgeois revolution shows the first manifestations of that spectrum of political parties from 'right-wing' via 'center' to 'left-wing' and 'leftists,' which became typical in later mature bourgeois revolutions. . . . The process of radicalization from 'right-wing' to 'left-wing' develops ideologically between the polarity of Luther and Müntzer; it develops politically and socially between a class constellation of princes, nobility, and urban burghers, on the one hand, and the rural-plebeian camp on the other."[10]

The period during which Karlstadt's work will be considered is the time between the Diet of Worms in 1521 and the outbreak of the Peasants' War. It is a period of the revolution which, on the one hand, gave further impetus to the movement of reform among broad segments of the people and, on the other hand, also made it clear that the forces involved in the revolution had diverse, partly conflicting social interests, political demands, and ideological views. In the period after the Diet of Worms, Luther's reforms attempted to consolidate the intellectual positions wrested from the old church in the years 1517-1521 and to reach an agreement with the political authorities about the practical consequences of reform. The radicalism of the early years began to give way to a centrist position. This meant the appeasement of the restless common people who pinned their hope for change in their everyday lives on the newly proclaimed and newly explained gospel. All reform measures which were carried out publicly were bound to cause a higher degree of public interest.

These correlations explain the events of the so-called Wittenberg Disturbances of 1521/22. What became evident at that time was the disagreement between Luther and Karlstadt. The latter, alongside others, comprehensively reformed worship at Wittenberg during Luther's stay at the Wartburg. Karlstadt celebrated the Eucharist under both kinds, abolished images in the

---

[10]Gerhard Brendler "Zur Bedeutung bürgerlicher Radikalität für Ideologie und Aktion Thomas Müntzers," in *Rolle und Formen der Volksbewegungen im bürgerlichen Revolutionszyklus*, ed. Martin Kossok (Berlin, 1976), 1.

churches, and proposed the creation of a Common Chest to resolve municipal social problems in a new way. This went hand in hand with a new order for begging that anticipated principles of modern bourgeois welfare[11], though in general it did not go beyond what Luther had advocated in his tract *An Open Letter To the Christian Nobility* of 1520. Luther's Invocavit Sermons denounced these innovations as too extensive—many of them were temporarily undone— and Karlstadt had to confine himself to his professorship at the university.[12] The fact that the Common Chest, the new order for begging, and the elimination of private Masses were affirmed suggests Luther's basic agreement with these measures as well as the economic interest of the Wittenberg burghers who benefited from these innovations. It was obviously of less concern that Luther reintroduced the Latin Mass, the vestments, and Communion under one kind only. Particularly suspect for Luther was Karlstadt's rigidity in carrying out reform, his strict reference to the Law, and his focus on the "common man" as the champion and benefactor of reform—tendencies which became more important for Karlstadt in subsequent years. Others involved in the Wittenberg events bowed to Luther's norm.

Karlstadt's notions of reform at Wittenberg—notions along the lines of apostolic Christianity—raised the issue of insurrection. One may take it for granted that he took a leading role in the deliberations of the University Committee which had been appointed to defend the Wittenberg reforms.[13] To be sure, the second opinion of the Committee rejected the charge that Karlstadt had incited uproar, but at the same time it was noted that, in connection with the introduction of the gospel, "such a great persecution [will] come over Christians as has not been known since the beginning of the world."[14] Scriptural proofs were presented to show that the desired reformation could not take place without disturbing the order of society.[15] In this context, there was no advocacy of the use of force, but the notion that governmental measures contradicting the introduction of the gospel should be ignored was not rejected. This meant latent conflict with the authorities. In his tract of July 29, 1521, *Report on this Saying: The Kingdom of Heaven Suffers Violence and the Rulers Take or Rob the Same*, Karlstadt expressed traces of similar thinking.[16] He

[11]See Andreas Karlstadt, "Von Abtuung der Bilder und das kein Bettler unter den Christen sein sollte," in *Flugschriften der frühen Reformationsbewegung (1518-1524)*, ed. Adolf Laube et al., (Berlin/Vaduz, 1983), 1:105-27; 2:1024-32. Karlstadt's ideas were immediately used in the "Ordnung der Stadt Wittenberg" (1522), ibid., 2:1033-37.

[12]Studies on the Wittenberg events are found in Preuss, Sider, Bubenheimer (all cited above) and in Martin Brecht's essay in *Martin Luther: Leben - Werk - Wirkung*, ed. Günter Vogler et al., (Berlin, 1983), 73-90.

[13]See Bubenheimer, "Aufruhr in Wittenberg," 184-86.

[14]Nikolaus Müller, "Die Wittenberger Bewegung" *Archiv für Reformationsgeschichte* 6 (1908/09): 279ff.   [15]Luke 2:34 was the reference used.

[16]C4a. See also the interpretation of Preuss, *Carlstadt's "Ordinaciones" and Luther's "Liberty,"* 14-17.

noted in the dedication that he was writing for the "simple-minded man" whom he urged to read the Bible frequently and to explain it to his children.[17] Karlstadt expressed this concern even more clearly in a tract on I Corinthians 1 which dealt with discord among brethren: "For the common people I say that I have hardly heard of anyone demanding the last penny from the parsons. They only ask that a Christian Mass and other proper evangelical worship be held."[18] What was touched upon here was the financial aspect of the celebration of the Mass. At that time Karlstadt's position with regard to public unrest and discussion and the common man's participation in the Reformation as a social event was different from, but not contrary to, Luther's position. One may agree with Bubenheimer who doubts that Luther approved of the events at Wittenberg until December 1521. With solid arguments, Bubenheimer dates Luther's *Faithful Admonition to all Christians to Guard Against Uproar and Rebellion* for December 1521 as a response to the events at Wittenberg of 1520/21.[19] It must remain uncertain if Luther knew Karlstadt's writings of 1521. Their sentiment, however, suggests that Karlstadt's participation in the reforms would not be surprising. The measures which he initiated and carried out entailed a radical continuation of reform and a criticism of the half-heartedness of the Lutheran movement with its strong commitment to the princes and the burghers. Karlstadt's radicalism grew out of the crisis of Luther's Reformation, on the one hand, and the escalating events of the revolution which were increasingly related to the action of the people on the other. His turn to the common people gave expression to this.

Even at Wittenberg, Karlstadt held positions whose sources were other than Luther's reform and which resulted in more radical attitudes. In 1520 Karlstadt included categories and ideas of medieval mysticism in his notion of reform and he did so on a more extensive scale than Luther. Although Luther published the *Theologia Deutsch*, its ideas did not become a crucial concern for him. But the mystic category *Gelassenheit* became decisive for Karlstadt and was the motif for his position, in the sense of a breaking away and separating from traditional conditions. As early as in his *Missive on the Supreme Virtue Gelassenheit* (October 11, 1520), which was dedicated to his mother and his friends, he pointed out, "I neither know father nor mother in this matter [i.e. the gospel]. I only follow the Scriptures which cannot be wrong . . . I want to get rid of my archdeaconate and all my belongings, . . . renounce father and mother, brother and sister, and let go everything, truly everything, in Gelassenheit of body and soul."[20] Karlstadt witnessed to this maxim by his

---

[17]A 1b.

[18]Sendbrief Andreas Bodenstein von Karlstadt, Erklärung Pauli: "Ich bitt' euch, Brüder, daß ihr allesamt eine Meinung reden wolltet," 1 Cor. 1, Wittenberg, 10 December 1521, sheet A3b.

[19]Bubenheimer, "Aufruhr in Wittenberg," 187-99.

[20]Karlstadt, *Missive*, B1b.

personal consequences. His first step was the rejection of the papacy which, until 1520, he had not repudiated as decisively as had Luther.[21] Subsequent events were his marriage to a former nun and the reforms at Wittenberg which went beyond Luther. In subsequent years, further consequences of a breaking away were the renunciation of his archdeaconate and his lectureship at the University, his work as a parson in Orlamünde, and eventually his work as peasant and shopkeeper. Measured by the values of his time, Karlstadt radically engaged in a decrease of status—not only under the pressure of external conditions but also in line with his own conviction to be closer to the "common man." Abandoning outward ceremonies and strictly referring to the Bible as Lex Dei he attempted to bring about a Christian lay piety in a reformed congregation, that is, he wanted to return to Christian roots. He was convinced that such a breaking away of man, his inward and outward restoration from routine, were necessary in order to create a truly new church, whose authentic function had been falsified over the centuries. The societal consequence was changed relationships among people. Karlstadt made the Christian commandment of charity into a law and—by resigning from positions of honor and office—no longer accepted the feudal class distinctions. Thereby he anticipated conceptions of the "heroic illusion" of the bourgeoisie which, centuries later, were reiterated in the slogan "Liberty, Equality, Fraternity." The Reformation showed incipient tendencies in this respect, but neither Luther nor the South German reformers expressed it as consistently as did Karlstadt.

In his *Missive on Gelassenheit* Karlstadt emphasized that there can be no peaceful introduction of the gospel. On the basis of Matthew 10 he noted that Christ came to send the sword which will cause pain.[22] Although he saw this largely as an intellectual process, he did include the real world as well. Karlstadt did not exclude the possibility of martyrdom for himself because he championed the new gospel, though he did not volunteer for it: "I am not particularly craving for the fire. That is why I will . . . flee from one town to the other."[23] Because of his new conviction he accepted punishment and persecution. He did not oppose them actively, but sought to evade by flight. His notion of reform did not include adaptation to prevailing conditions, but meant unrest, confrontation, and schism. This basic notion remained unchanged in his writings of 1522-24. He confirmed it in 1523 in a major tract on *Gelassenheit*,[24] though with few references to his own historical situation. An essential reason for Luther's rejection of Karlstadt, I believe, lies

---

[21]Karlstadt, *Von päpstlicher Heiligkeit*, October 17, 1520.

[22]Karlstadt, *Missive*, B1b-B2a.

[23]Ibid., sheet B3a.

[24]*Was gesagt ist, sich gelassen* April 20 1523, with the addition: "Andreas Bodenstein von Karlstadt, ein neuer Laie."

precisely in this propensity of Karlstadt's reform which found expression in differing attitudes. It brought Karlstadt and his work in Wittenberg, Orlamünde, and Rothenburg in contact with more radical bourgeois classes and encouraged their opposition against the authorities. A sharper analysis from the perspective of the history of ideology of Karlstadt's reception of mysticism with its relevance for practical life is needed and calls for further research, even though initial studies are available.[25] This might lead to a clearer understanding of his latent notions of insurrection and a sharpening of Luther's concept of the *Schwärmer.* C. A. Pater, in an interesting way, has linked Karlstadt's mystically influenced views of sanctification as conquest of the self through divine grace with his application of the Mosaic Law to the social sphere. Incipient notions of a radical change of society can be discerned.[26]

The tendency toward a type of passive resistance is obvious in Karlstadt's attitude during his stay at Orlamünde. Although the congregation appreciated his reform of the liturgy and the municipal social welfare system, his superiors, the chapter and the University, prevented his official appointment and provoked the Elector to action. Still, Karlstadt remained in the parish. Indeed, he stressed his loyalty to the Elector, but also emphasized that he was more subservient to God, even, if necessary, against the Elector's will. Moreover, he expressed his conviction that the true Gospel was not preached at Wittenberg.[27] In a letter to the Elector, Spalatin noted that "Karlstadt continues to gain ground every day with his seductive, ungodly, and even seditious tenets . . . which will lead, provided this is not countered, to great disaster."[28] Indeed, in the spring of 1524 Karlstadt established contacts with several small Thuringian towns, such as Allstedt and Kahla, and with Jena. The danger of a counter-Wittenberg was real.

What was considered particularly offensive in Wittenberg was that Karlstadt no longer baptized infants. In his *Missive,* noted earlier, he hinted that man becomes regenerated through "inward anguish."[29] The sacrament of Baptism was spiritualized. Karlstadt sharply distinguished between act and symbol, a distinction which illustrated his understanding of the other sacraments as well, especially the Eucharist. The rejection of the real presence of

[25]See also Sider, *Andreas Bodenstein von Karlstadt,* 74-201.

[26]Calvin Augustin Pater, "Kritische Stellungnahme zu Luthers Karlstadt-Bild," in *Ökumenische Erschließung Martin Luthers,* ed. Peter Manns and H. Meyer (Paderborn/Frankfurt a.M., 1983), 250-58. For the dimensions of Luther's thoughts about the radicals see Günther Mühlpfordt, "Luther und die 'Linken' – Eine Untersuchung seiner Schwärmerterminologie," in *Martin Luther: Leben - Werk - Wirkung,* 325-45.

[27]Karlstadt to Elector Frederick, May 22, 1524 in E. Hase, "Karlstadt in Orlamünde," *Mitteilungen der geschichts- und altertumsforschenden Gesellschaft des Osterlandes* 4 (1858): 106.

[28]Ibid., 111. Spalatin to the Elector Frederick, after May 28, 1524.

[29]Karlstadt, *Missive,* A3a.

Christ in the Lord's Supper precipitated a widespread controversy which proved particularly aggravating in light of the political situation in 1524. The discontinuance of infant baptism, like the reform of the social welfare system, challenged societal traditions. The baptismal ceremony was considered to represent integration into the Christian community as well as the confession of subordination to a legally structured community. Leaving baptism to the discretion of the individual meant a degree of freedom that could be injurious to the political order. This view, too, gives Karlstadt's position a radical tinge.

The Communion controversy showed another distinctiveness of Karlstadt's which also denoted his limited willingness to compromise. From fall and winter of 1524 to the spring of 1525 he stood always ready to discuss basic theological issues and in so doing to involve wide circles of laymen. By that date Luther's Reformation had already begun to establish and petrify its doctrine. For Karlstadt, on the other hand, the reform movement was still open to change.

The Strasbourg episode of early October 1524 clearly illustrated this point of view. During his four-day stay in the city Karlstadt did not call on the leading preachers Bucer, Capito, Hedio, and others, but stayed with Otto Brunfels who occupied a unique position among the adherents of the Reformation in Strasbourg. Karlstadt talked with lay preachers, such as the gardener Clemens Ziegler, and won them over to his views. The City Council later spoke of a "sect which was organized by Karlstadt for the sake of the sacrament among the common people."[30] The Strasbourg preachers who cooperated closely with the reform-minded party on the Council[31] were not particularly enthusiastic about Karlstadt's visit because he avoided them and did not discuss his views with them. They disassociated themselves from him, particularly because of his impatience in implementing evangelical reform and his endorsement of iconoclasm even in the absence of the authorities' consent—a specific charge levied against him by Capito, who deplored the division in the reform movement. In light of the consolidation of the counter-reform movement, the ruthless measures of some authorities against the Reformation on the grounds of the Edict of Worms, and the beginning peasants' uprising, such internal disagreement was bound to have incalculable consequences. The Strasbourg reformers shared Luther's notion that it was necessary to carry out ecclesiastical change slowly, deliberately, and with the consent of the political authorities—or with regard for the "weak in faith."[32] Initially, they generally

---

[30]J. Rott, Quellen zur Geschichte der Täufer, Elsaß I, Nr. 30, p. 44. See also Sigrid Looß, "Zu einigen Aspekten des Verhältnisses zwischen Luther und Karlstadt, vorwiegend dargestellt an Karlstadts Straßburgaufenthalt im Oktober 1524," Protokollband der Zentralen Lutherkonferenz (Berlin, 1983), 142-47.

[31]See Sigrid Looß, "Reformatorische Ideologie und Praxis im Dienst des Rates und der Bürgerschaft Straßburgs," Jahrbuch für Geschichte des Feudalismus 5 (Berlin, 1981): 255-90.

[32]Wolfgang Capito, Was man halten soll..., A2b; A4a.

did not proceed from theological, but from political considerations. Concerning Communion the South Germans later approximated Karlstadt's position. The reaction of the Strasbourg preachers anticipated the rejection of Karlstadt's tract *If One Should Tarry*[33] of November 1524. In this tract Karlstadt reiterated his views regarding speedy ecclesiastical change. His presence in Strasbourg resulted in division. The Strasbourg preachers faced the reality of divisiveness in their own ranks in the context of a politically and socially restless situation in town and Empire. They were forced to consider and discuss basic theological premises. Their uncertainty with regard to theological issues and to questions of practical church reform prompted more vigorous manifestations of self-confidence on the part of more radical elements, such as Ziegler, Denck, Kautz, and others which substantially paved the way for the beginning of Anabaptism and furthered the division of the Reformation. In Strasbourg, Karlstadt's intellectual criticism of Luther precipitated a split into followers of Luther (Grebel), a mediating group (Capito and Bucer), and followers of Karlstadt (Brunfels, Ziegler).[34]

An important aspect in the analysis of Karlstadt's radicalism was also his stay in Rothenburg from January to late May 1525. He wrote several tracts, among them the important *Main Articles of Christian Doctrine*, a response to Luther's *Against the Heavenly Prophets*, which included an analysis of Luther's teaching of the two kingdoms.[35] Karlstadt stressed—in his *Apology* of June 24, 1525[36]—that he was not responsible for the events of the Peasants' War in and around Rothenburg and he emphasized his role as a mediator between the parties in conflict, although the relationship between cause and effect in connection with his presence and the events in Rothenburg have not as yet been thoroughly analyzed. Karlstadt's own statement indicates that he got between the parties in May 1525 and that flight was the only way out. But it is necessary to examine in greater detail Karlstadt's influence on the urban opposition in the time prior to May 1525. This would include the question of the character of the reform in Rothenburg after March 25 when a committee of the opposition resolved matters, formed an alliance with the peasants, and even provided military aid. One thing is clear: Karlstadt, through his connec-

---

[33]Text in E. Hertzsch, ed., *Karlstadts Schriften aus den Jahren 1523-1525*, Part 1, (Halle, 1956), 70-97.

[34]A more detailed new study concerning Karlstadt's relationship to the South Germans in general has yet to come. Calvin A. Pater examines the links with Zwingli, Melchior Hoffman, and the Swiss Anabaptists in *Karlstadt as the Father of the Baptist Movement* (Toronto: Toronto University Press, 1984); see also Klaus Deppermann, *Melchior Hoffman: Soziale Unruhen und apokalyptische Visionen im Zeitalter der Reformation* (Göttingen, 1979), 149-55; H. W. Müssing, "Karlstadt und die Entstehung der Straßburger Täufergemeinde," in *Les débuts et les characteristiques de l'anabaptisme*, ed. Marc Lienhard (The Hague, 1977), 169-95.

[35]Andreas Karlstadt, "Anzeige etlicher Hauptartikel christlicher Lehre," in *Karlstadts Schriften*, Part 2, pp. 94-102.

[36]Ibid., 105-18.

tion with the urban opposition, got into opposition with the old Council. Barge's comprehensive biography of Karlstadt does not sufficiently note that the leaders of the urban opposition were brought to trial after the Battle of Königshofen because of their relationship with Karlstadt. Several were executed.[37] The recent suggestion that Karlstadt wrote the anonymous revolutionary pamphlet *To the Assembly of the Common Peasants*[38] makes the need to deal with this complex of issues imperative. A close friend of Karlstadt's in Rothenburg, the schoolmaster Valentin Ickelschamer, stated the position of the Karlstadt Party against Luther: "Christians are rough fellows . . . they tell the truth and are hotspurs in full measure . . . they wear disgraceful habits. Well, dear Luther, you will remain a monk because you despise and dislike the peasants . . . Everywhere there are too many poor, they do not have anything to eat and that is why Christ left a small and trifling possession to the preachers."[39] This reminds us of Karlstadt's basic position with respect to a modest conduct of life and his orientation toward the common people. This placed him and his followers to the "left" of Luther. Karlstadt objected to the use of force by the peasants against their rulers which he witnessed in Rothenburg. An alliance which Allstedt offered Orlamünde did not come to fruition because of Karlstadt's influence. In his letters to Müntzer, Karlstadt tried to dissuade him from organizing rebellion.[40] It must be noted that during Karlstadt's stay at Orlamünde his intellectual kinship with Müntzer was such that Müntzer still considered Karlstadt and his congregation as appropriate allies even after he had broken with Luther. There are indications that Karlstadt was inclined to passive resistance, a notion which proved to be open to further development.

In conclusion, I want to return to my initial questions which relate to Karlstadt's place in the course of the Reformation. Luther's Reformation is a valid norm for assessing Karlstadt and his views; it is the yardstick for Karlstadt's radical positions. Through his role in a reform movement which was to be part of a larger social process, Karlstadt participated, more drastically than Luther, in bringing about change and influencing opposition currents and attitudes between 1521 and 1525. In so doing Karlstadt did not openly oppose the prevailing structures molded by the authorities, but he enhanced the latent opposition by disregarding official pronouncements. In Strasbourg

---

[37]See Barge, 2: 297-357. See also Justus Maurer "Karlstadt und der Bauernkrieg," *Andreas Bodenstein v. Karlstadt* (Karlstadt, 1980), 105ff.

[38]Christian Peters, "An die Versammlung gemeiner Bauerschaft (1525)," *Zeitschrift für bayrische Kirchengeschichte* 54 (1985): 16-28.

[39]Valentin Ickelshamer, "Klage etlicher Brüder...1525," *Flugschriften der Reformationszeit* 10 (Halle, 1983): 46.

[40]"Der von Orlamünde Schrift an die zu Allstedt," *Flugschriften der frühen Reformationsbewegung*, 1: 443-45. Karlstadt's Letter to Müntzer of July 19, 1524 in Gütersloh, 1968), 415ff.

and Rothenburg he was catalyst of the movement. His behavior lays bare contradictions and different fractions. It appears that he was an integrative figure for a certain group of bourgeois intellectuals (Martin Reinhart, Gerhard Westerburg, Valentin Ickelschamer, Otto Brunfels). His rigidity in church reform and his personal attitude and conduct of life converge with the interests of non-privileged bourgeois classes and the intellectuals who concluded that Luther's bourgeois Reformation had come to an abortive standstill. Until the Peasants' War they wanted to involve the "common people" more intensely in the Reformation movement. This attitude expressed resignation and a modification of the notion to bring about universal change in church and state with the help of the authorities. The outbreak of the Peasants' War made the consequences alarmingly clear to these more radical bourgeois forces. They no longer shared this escalation of radicalism. The function of this group, i.e. to advance the movement of reform by latent and public criticism, had been fulfilled with the outbreak of the Peasants' War. The reception of Karlstadt's ideas in the Anabaptist movement belongs to a changed social context and is therefore outside the topic of this paper.

Thomas Müntzer, Preacher to Alstedt in Düringen.
Woodcut by Christoph (Karl?) van Sichen

Thomas Müntzer and Luther:
A Tragedy of Errors

Eric W. Gritsch

THE THEME "MÜNTZER AND LUTHER" has remained controversial ever since Karl Holl tackled it in his well-known essay of 1922,[1] in the context of the problem of "Luther and the *Schwärmer*." According to Holl, Müntzer was a Luther disciple who so integrated what he received from Luther with his own creative thought that in the end he became the prototypical opponent of the Wittenberg reformer. As such, he not only coined all the *Schwärmer* slogans but has also remained the leading *Geist* of a radical movement ranging from Anabaptists to the Anglo-American sects that emphasized voluntary *Gemeinschaft*, human rights, and a hope for the Kingdom of God on earth.

A Research Labyrinth

Holl's basic thesis has been challenged in the light of new evidence, particularly with regard to Müntzer's historical impact (*Wirkungsgeschichte*). Müntzer's link to Luther has remained one of the most enduring problems in the massive research on Müntzer since Holl.[2]

General biographies grant some dependence of Müntzer on Luther, but vary in their assessment of its importance. The 1947 biography by the Russian historian M. M. Smirin depicts Müntzer as the founder of a "people's reformation (*Volksreformation*)" which, in contrast to "Luther's Party (*Luthers Partei*)," advocated a socio-political revolution that would begin with the rebellion of the peasants. According to Smirin, Müntzer already began to challenge Luther in Zwickau in 1520 and—under the influence of Joachim of Fiore, late medieval mysticism, and Taborite eschatology—developed his own theology of revolution. Smirin leans towards the thesis that Müntzer was a mystic, but he does not make clear to what degree Müntzer was truly dependent on mysticism or Joachimite-Taborite eschatology. Smirin claims that Luther was, at best, an early ally.[3]

[1] Karl Holl, "Luther und die Schwärmer," *Gesammelte Aufsätze zur Kirchengeschichte*, 2 vols., 5th ed. (Tübingen, 1927), 1:420-67. For a critical appraisal of Holl, see Eric W. Gritsch, "Luther und die Schwärmer: Verworfene Anfechtung?" *Luther* 47 (1976): 105-21.

[2] See the bibliography in Eric W. Gritsch, *Reformer Without a Church: The Life and Thought of Thomas Müntzer, 1488?-1525* (Philadelphia: Fortress Press, 1967). A useful evaluation of Müntzer texts and secondary literature is offered by Siegfried Bräuer, "Müntzerforschung von 1965 bis 1975," *Lutherjahrbuch* 44 (1977): 127-41; *Lutherjahrbuch* 45 (1978): 102-29. See also Hans J. Hillerbrand, *Thomas Müntzer: a Bibliography* (St. Louis: Center for Reformation Research, 1976).

[3] M. M. Smirin, *Die Volksreformation des Thomas Müntzers und der grosse deutsche Bauernkrieg*, 2d ed. (Berlin, 1956), esp. pp. 88-89 and chs. 2-4.

My own 1967 biography pointed to the period from May 1520 to April 1521, when Müntzer resided in Zwickau and struggled with Catholics and with the Humanist preacher Johann Egranus, as the time he broke with Luther; and I assessed the theological differences between Müntzer and Luther in the light of their treatments of the authority of the "word" (scriptural, proclaimed, and sacramentally enacted) and of the "spirit" (the experiencing of the Holy Spirit without external means).[4]

In his biographical study of 1969, E. Gordon Rupp suggested that "perhaps" Müntzer "begins to leave the Martinian camp" in the Spring of 1522; and that "in July 1523, then, Müntzer ceased to be a Martinian." But Rupp's occasional hints concerning the theological differences between Müntzer and Luther indicate no firm conclusions.[5]

Walter Elliger's massive work of 1975 depicts Müntzer as a Luther disciple who combined what he learned from Luther with his own quest for the restitution of apostolic Christianity. But Elliger's summation of Müntzer's link to Luther is clothed in complex, and indeed unclear, language: he stated that Müntzer was a Luther disciple "who, to be sure, already came to Wittenberg with the bias (*Voreingenommenheit*) of an independent and personal formulation of questions (*Fragestellung*), and heard and assimilated 'the new teaching' of the 'young Luther' in this context. . . . Luther made the radical break, not Müntzer, even though it was he [Müntzer] who had already separated himself from him [Luther]."[6]

Eike Wohlgast's 1981 biography only deals with general differences between Müntzer and Luther, focusing on their differences regarding the relationship of "word" and "spirit."[7]

The 1983 Marxist biography by Manfred Bensing is unclear about Müntzer's link to Luther, stating that Müntzer was an "ally (*Bundesgenosse*)" who admired and supported Luther without, however, ever having become dependent on him. Bensing also points to the plurality of social and intellec-

---

[4]Gritsch, *Reformer Without a Church*, 27-38. Based on the work of Paul Wappler, *Thomas Müntzer in Zwickau und die "Zwickauer Propheten,"* 2d. ed. rev. (Gütersloh, 1966), I overestimated the influence of Nicholas Storch. But Wappler saw more evidence than was actually there. See Siegfried Bräuer, "Müntzers Weg in den Bauernkrieg" in *Thomas Müntzer. Anfragen an die Theologie und Kirche*, ed. Christoph Demke (Berlin, 1977), 66, 81 n6.

[5]Gordon Rupp, *Patterns of Reformation* (Philadelphia: Fortress Press, 1969), 182-83, 188, 263, 266.

[6]Walter Elliger, *Thomas Müntzer. Leben und Werk* (Göttingen, 1975), 7. See also the summary of the book under the title *Aussenseiter der Reformation: Thomas Müntzer* (Göttingen, 1975), 5-7. Elliger's German is, at times, intensively ambiguous: "Den radikalen Bruch vollzog Luther, nicht Müntzer, obschon dieser es war, der sich bereits von ihm getrennt hatte" (p. 7). That Elliger's work does not represent the final word on Müntzer has been clearly demonstrated by the reviewer Siegfried Bräuer in *Theologische Literaturzeitung* 102 (1977): 215-20.

[7]Eike Wohlgast, *Thomas Müntzer. Ein Verstörer der Ungläubigen. Persönlichkeit und Geschichte* (Göttingen, 1981).

tual concerns engendering various views of what "reform" could be. But how influential any of these views were for Müntzer, and how much influence Luther had on him, remain an open question.[8]

The most recent German biographical sketches of Müntzer tend to ascribe more significance to the influence of mysticism on Müntzer than any decisive influence Luther may have had on him. According to Siegfried Bräuer and Hans-Jürgen Goertz, the "first beginnings (*Ansatz*)" of Müntzer's "theology of revolution" can be traced to "grades of tradition (*Traditionsgefälle*)" in medieval mysticism; to the apocalyptic "milieu" created by Joachimite eschatological speculations and by Taborite chiliasm; and to the early writings of Luther, "in the way in which Müntzer understood them." But both authors explain that Müntzer's thoughts were "erratic (*sprunghaft*)" and "associative (*assoziativ*)"; that the sources of his piety and argumentation can rarely be ascertained; and that the motives for his actions are not always clear.[9]

Ulrich Bubenheimer thinks that Müntzer developed his views, especially his anti-Roman Catholic stance, without the influence of Luther, because he had been a successful theological critic of indulgences in Braunschweig before Luther's Ninety-Five Theses appeared in 1517. At that time, Müntzer's friends had already been calling him "persecutor of unrighteousness," a title which, according to Bubenheimer, shows that Müntzer's basic stance as a reformer "has 'pre-reformation' roots." If Luther and Müntzer had anything in common, according to Bubenheimer, it was their coat-of-arms: both displayed a heart in the center, symbolizing what had come to be known as "the heart of Jesus mysticism (*Herz Jesu-Mystik*)." But how Müntzer dealt with Luther's problem of "Word and Spirit," to which Müntzer was attuned, remains a question.[10]

Special studies of the relationship between Müntzer and Luther are equally inconclusive. In 1955, Hayo Gerdes amplified Holl's thesis regarding Müntzer's dependence on Luther by comparing their understanding of "the way of faith."[11] According to Gerdes, Müntzer had distanced himself from Luther by 1522, when he began to preach about the imminent end of the world and the need to restore apostolic Christianity; he had learned from Luther about the inner turmoil (*Anfechtung*) of Christians still plagued by sin,

[8]Manfred Bensing, *Thomas Müntzer*, 3d. ed. rev. (Leipzig, 1983), 30.

[9]Siegfried Bräuer and Hans-Jürgen Goertz, "Thomas Müntzer" in *Gestalten der Kirchengeschichte*, ed. Martin Greschat, vol. 5, *Die Reformationszeit* 1 (Stuttgart, 1981), 347.

[10]Ulrich Bubenheimer, "Thomas Müntzer" in *Protestantische Profile*, ed. Klaus Scholder and Dieter Kleinmann (Königstein, Ts., 1983), 36-37. See also his essay,"Thomas Müntzer und der Anfang der Reformation in Braunschweig," *Nederlands Archief voor Kerkgeschiedenis* 65 (1985): 1-29. Müntzer's involvement in reforms in Braunschweig before 1517 is difficult to assess in the light of sparse sources. See Siegfried Bräuer, "Thomas Müntzers Beziehungen zur Braunschweiger Frühreformation," *Theologische Literaturzeitung* 109 (1984): 636-38.

[11]Hayo Gerdes,"Der Weg des Glaubens bei Müntzer und Luther," *Luther* 25 (1955): 152-63.

law, and death; in the end, he differed from Luther in his attitude to the world (he called for the forceful removal of the godless), in his understanding of sanctification, and in his concept of the relationship of word and spirit. But Gerdes did not discuss specific details concerning these major differences, and he rather uncritically reaffirmed Luther's position.

In 1961, Carl Hinrichs compared Luther's and Müntzer's views of political authority and the individual's right to resist.[12] Based on an analysis of Müntzer's last three treatises, Hinrichs depicted Luther and Müntzer as classic opponents who had virtually nothing in common. Without any critical evaluation of Holl, Hinrichs simply sketched the story of Müntzer as the defeat of the Allstedt reformer who had tried to replace Luther as the leader of a reform movement that failed to care for the common people. In Hinrichs' portrayal, Müntzer appears to have been Luther's great rival; but Hinrichs offers no major clue as to Luther's real influence on Müntzer.

In 1963, Thomas Nipperdey amplified Holl's thesis regarding Müntzer's dependence on Luther by contending that Luther was Müntzer's "basic theological problem (*sein theologisches Grundproblem*)."[13] According to Nipperdey, Müntzer turned Luther's theology upside-down, as it were, beginning with the word/spirit dialectic: focusing on the subjective experiencing of the Holy Spirit, he transformed Luther's theology of justification into a theology of sanctification that views the "inspired" believer as an activist who changes a sinful world into an obedient covenant society of the last days before the end-time—thus the connection between theology and revolution. Granting the influence of Taborite eschatology and medieval mysticism on Müntzer, Nipperdey nevertheless holds fast to the thesis that Müntzer's theology is anchored in "a radical subjectivising" of Luther's theology of justification; and, in his 1974 Addendum, he saw no reason to change his mind in the light of later research.[14]

In 1967, Hans-Jürgen Goertz attempted to show that Müntzer's views are totally grounded in medieval mysticism and its dialectic of internal and external order.[15] Müntzer joined in Luther's initial attack against Rome, but he

---

[12]Carl Hinrichs, *Luther und Müntzer. Ihre Auseinandersetzung über Obrigkeit und Widerstandsrecht* (Berlin, 1962).

[13]Thomas Nipperdey, "Theologie und Revolution bei Thomas Müntzer," *Archiv für Reformationsgeschichte* 54 (1963): 145-79. Reprinted in Th. Nipperdey, *Reformation, Revolution, Utopie. Studien zum 16. Jahrhundert* (Göttingen, 1975), 38-75. Quotations pp. 40, 47. On the differences with Luther, pp. 57-64.

[14]Ibid., 83-84.

[15]Hans-Jürgen Goertz, *Innere und äussere Ordnung in der Theologie Thomas Müntzers* (Leiden, 1967), esp. 25-28. English summary in Goertz, "Thomas Müntzer: Revolutionary in a Mystical Spirit," in *Profiles of Radical Reformers. Biographical Sketches from Thomas Müntzer to Paracelsus*, ed. H.-J. Goertz and Walther Klaassen (Scottdale, Pa.: Herald Press, 1982), 29-44. See some modifications of the basic thesis in Goertz, "Der Mystiker mit dem Hammer," *Kerygma und Dogma* 20 (1974): 23-53.Goertz argues against the thesis that there is a link between Luther's notion of

already did so on the basis of a "mystical spiritualism" which he revealed for the first time during his debate with Egranus in Zwickau. He used the mystical thought form of "the order of God" to dedicate his life and work to the restitution of this original unity, lost through human sin, between God and the human soul. Once the "inner order" is restored in the believer, the world's "external order" can be transformed into an appropriate covenant of obedience to God, and this transformation will be accomplished by a cadre of the elect organized by Müntzer and poised to attack the sinful external structures of the world—thus the link between theology and revolution.

Both Nipperdey and Goertz tried to find a *Leitmotif* whereby they could reconstruct the "live" Müntzer. They arrived at radically different conclusions: Nipperdey made Müntzer into an anticipator of modern movements; Goertz labeled Müntzer the "custodian (*Verwalter*)" of what is past.[16] Both are open to the charge of underestimating the pluriformity of early Reformation theology, which did not originate with just Luther or with adherents to medieval mysticism.[17]

Heiko A. Oberman has called attention to the democratic trends in late medieval mysticism, and tried to show how Müntzer was attracted to them as well as to the anti-scholastic Pauline-Augustinian theology prevalent in Wittenberg from 1516 to 1520. According to Oberman, Müntzer also related the young Luther's notion of faith, described in terms of bride-mysticism, to his own interest in predestination, and finally argued for "the great sorting out (*de grote scheiding*)"—first microcosmically in heart and soul, then macrocosmically in world and history. Thus Oberman agreed with Goertz, and suggested an interesting link between mysticism and political history in Müntzer's theology.[18]

Wolfgang Rochler, on the other hand, did disagree with Goertz. He demonstrated that Müntzer, in arriving at a theology of judgment, had used the mystical notion of "order" in the context of "covenant," rather than

Anfechtung and Müntzer's mysticism. See Martin Schmidt, "Das Selbstbewusstsein Thomas Müntzers und sein Verhältnis zu Luther. Ein Beitrag zu der Frage: War Thomas Müntzer ein Mystiker?," *Theologia Viatorum* (1954/58): 25-41, esp. 40. That Luther was the radical and Müntzer the medieval conservative, is also argued, in support of Goertz and against Nipperdey, by Carter Lindberg, "Theology and Politics: Luther the Radical and Müntzer the Reaction," *Encounter* 37 (1976): 356-71.

[16]Nipperdey rejects the notion that Müntzer is "medieval" ("Both are no longer medieval") and views him as the critical thinker who anticipates the weaknesses of post-Reformation Lutheranism (orthodoxy, political passivity, individualism) and represents theocratic violence. (Nipperdey, *Reformation, Revolution*, 84). See Goertz, *Innere und äussere Ordnung*, 149.

[17]See Bräuer, "Müntzerforschung," 128.

[18]Heiko A. Oberman, "Thomas Müntzer: van verontrusting tot verzert," *Kerk en Theologie* 24 (1973): 205-14. esp. 210. See also Steven E. Ozment, "Thomas Müntzer" in *Mysticism and Dissent. Religious Ideology and Social Protest in the Sixteenth Century* (New Haven: Yale University Press, 1973), 61-97.

"creation" as Goertz claimed.[19] Gottfried Maron had arrived at a similar view, arguing that Müntzer's "theology of judgment" was derived from the Bible rather than from just medieval mysticism.[20]

Reinhard Schwarz also rejected the thesis that Müntzer was decisively influenced by medieval mysticism. Instead, Schwarz linked Müntzer to Taborite eschatology, which, as a "complex of chiliastic ideas (*chiliastischer Ideenkomplex*)," had also influenced the young Luther. "Müntzer's theology and activities cannot be understood as long as Luther's influence and that of mysticism or that of the chiliastic Taborite tradition are played against each other." Schwarz concluded that all these factors produced a "peculiar fusion (*eigentümliche Verschmelzung*)" in Müntzer's thought and action, not unrelated to Luther's theology. But Schwarz does not offer definite conclusions as to the degree of Luther's influence on Müntzer.[21]

In 1974, Bernhard Lohse dealt with the theme "Luther and Müntzer" by analyzing their theological development from 1520 to 1525. According to Lohse, they were favorably impressed with each other when they met in 1518, but Müntzer used the thought forms of late medieval mysticism, echoed late medieval piety regarding suffering and discipleship, and developed an eschatology that differed from that of Luther. Lohse concluded that, in light of Goertz's work, Müntzer can no longer be viewed as a disciple of Luther, but must be seen as an independent thinker who developed a consistent "spirit-revolution (*Geistrevolution*)" over against Luther's Bible-faith (*Bibelglaube*)." In the end, Luther must be judged as being both realistic and correct in his views, even though Müntzer's commitment to human need remains a question at issue for the church at any time.[22]

In 1975, Max Steinmetz, the dean of Marxist Reformation research, rejected the thesis that Luther influenced Müntzer, contending that Müntzer's thought was anchored in the "class struggles" of 1521 to 1525. He summa-

---

[19]Wolfgang Rochler, "Ordnungsbegriff und Gottesgedanke bei Thomas Müntzer," *Zeitschrift für Kirchengeschichte* 85 (1974): 369-82, esp. 371-72.

[20]Gottfried Maron, "Thomas Müntzer als Theologe des Gerichts: Das 'Urteil'—ein Schlüsselbegriff seines Denkens," *Zeitschrift für Kirchengeschichte* 83 (1972): 195-225. See also his rather uncritical comparison of Müntzer and Luther in "Thomas Müntzer in der Sicht Luthers," *Theologia Viatorum* 12 (1973): 71-85. Goertz softened his stance in the light of such criticism, declaring that Müntzer had appropriated the "practical" rather than the "speculative" part of mysticism as "the building block (*Aufbauelement*) of his theology"; and other influences could also be detected, such as "Hussite-Taborite and eschatological-apocalyptic splinters of thought (*Gedankensplitter*)." All of this is also related to what Müntzer heard from the reformers. See Goertz, "Der Mystiker mit dem Hammer," 31.

[21]Reinhard Schwarz, *Die apokalyptische Theologie Thomas Müntzers und der Taboriten* (Tübingen, 1977), 125-26.

[22]Bernhard Lohse, "Luther und Müntzer," *Luther* 44 (1974): 12-32, esp. 17, 31-32. See also the attempt to show that Müntzer may have broken away from Luther as early as 1519 when he was in Jüterbog: Shinzo Tanaka, "Eine Seite der geistigen Entwicklung Thomas Müntzers in seiner 'lutherischen' Zeit," *Lutherjahrbuch* 40 (1973): 76-88, esp. 86-87.

rized the differences between Müntzer and Luther by elaborating what he considered to be the basic components of the theology Müntzer formulated in his struggle against Luther's social and political "passivity": a doctrine of the Holy Spirit no longer bound to the authority of the Bible; a doctrine of the cross manifested in spiritual suffering and in purification for the sake of "true faith"; and a doctrine of the sword which claimed the right to resist godless authority and to bring justice to the poor and the oppressed.[23]

In 1976, Helmar Junghans compared Müntzer and Luther in a study of their views of faith. In this study, Müntzer's view appeared to be anchored in a neo-Platonic world-view adopted by Dominican mysticism and evidenced in a concept of faith as "substance (*Glaubensstoff*)," as *fides infusa*.[24] Junghans tried to show how Müntzer, from this perspective, rejected Luther's claim that salvation comes through externals like the preached word and the enacted sacraments, and that their theological debate echoed the medieval quarrel between "realists" and "conceptualists," thus reviving the old conflict between Platonists and Aristotelians. But Junghans conceded that it is difficult to demonstrate this on the basis of the literary evidence.[25]

In 1978, Leif Grane warned against the tendency to transform a historical person into a type representing a certain way of thinking, and offered some basic insights: Müntzer and Luther had a good relationship until 1522, at which time Müntzer began to suspect the Wittenbergers of compromising what he perceived to be the Word of God; at the same time, Luther was losing patience with those he deemed weak and ready to rebel against political authority; the chief theological issue between them was the interpretation of the law of Moses, for Müntzer used it to justify violence; both men were already going their separate ways before the Peasants' War of 1525. According to Grane, Müntzer was essentially a preacher who used the biblical word with great creativity to proclaim the coming of a new world; linked to the Peasants' War, such proclamation spurred Luther to renounce his original notion of letting the Word of God ream freely, and thus he paved the way for a territorial "state church (*obrigkeitliche Kirche*)" without knowing what he did, "and perhaps also without wishing to do so."[26]

In 1984, Marianne Schaub compared Müntzer and Luther in the context of "divine right" and "princely absolutism." According to Schaub, Müntzer linked the divine promise of salvation to the individual's right to use the sword to separate the children of God and the godless, and thus rejected the political

[23]Max Steinmetz, "Thomas Müntzer in der Forschung der Gegenwart," *Zeitschrift für Geschichtswissenschaft* 23 (1975): 665-85, esp. 676.

[24]Helmar Junghans, "Ursachen für das Glaubensverständnis Thomas Müntzers 1524," in *Der deutsche Bauernkrieg und Thomas Müntzer*, ed. Max Steinmetz (Leipzig, 1976), 148.

[25]Ibid., 149.

[26]Leif Grane, "Thomas Müntzer und Martin Luther," in *Thomas Müntzer und Martin Luther*, ed. Abraham Friesen and Hans-Jürgen Goertz (Darmstadt, 1975), 74-111, esp. 87, 100.

hierarchy of princes that Luther defended. Although Schaub compares the theological reflections of the two reformers—focusing on "incarnation" and "scriptural authority"—she offers no conclusions with regard to the origins of Müntzer's ideas.[27]

In quest of a scholarly consensus on the theme "Müntzer and Luther," one discovers instead a labyrinth of research. Is there a way out of this labyrinth? One can only follow the path of primary sources and once again ask: did Müntzer understand himself to be a disciple of Luther? If so, for how long? If not, why did some of his contemporaries call him a "Martinian"? What did Luther say about Müntzer? Why did he attack him? The answers must obviously be sought in Müntzer's and Luther's writings. But whereas the Luther corpus yields relatively clear answers, the Müntzer torso is still in a stage of reconstruction.[28] Its lacunae on a variety of subjects, including Müntzer's attitude towards Luther, tempt scholars to speculate and to use theological, political, social, psycho-historical and other methods to arrive at conclusions regarding the origins and impact of Müntzer's life and work (*Entstehungs-Wirkungsgeschichte*).

There may simply not be enough evidence to speak the final word on Müntzer. But there is a need to make another attempt to deal with the question of Müntzer's attitude towards Luther and to examine Luther's judgment of Müntzer in light of evidence on Müntzer's side. This paper will first examine the evidence contained in the primary sources and then use the findings to draw some conclusions regarding the relationship between the two men.

The Müntzer Evidence

Müntzer's first contact with Luther may have been made in 1518, during his stay of perhaps a few months in Wittenberg.[29] By that time Luther had become well-known through his Ninety-Five Theses and through his curricular reforms at Wittenberg University.

---

[27]Marianne Schaub, *Müntzer Contre Luther. Le droit divin contre l'absolutisme Princier* (Paris, 1985), esp. Part 3. See also the general comparison of Müntzer and Luther in the context of a refutation of Ernst Bloch's "socialist" view of Luther: Iris Geyer, *Thomas Müntzer im Bauernkrieg. Analyse zweier seiner Hauptschriften unter Berücksichtigung des sozial-geistesgeschichtlichen Hintergrunds. Ernst Bloch's zeit- und ideologiebedingtes Missverständnis, Thomas Müntzer betreffend* (Bensingheim, 1982), esp. 25-28.

[28]Most of Müntzer's writings are available in Günther Franz, ed., *Thomas Müntzer: Schriften und Briefe. Kritische Gesamtausgabe* (Gütersloh, 1968). Hereafter cited as *MKG*. This edition is not without faults. See the critique by Siegfried Bräuer, "Die erste Gesamtausgabe von Thomas Müntzer Schriften und Briefe," *Lutherjahrbuch* 38 (1971): 129-131; and idem, "Müntzerforschung." A team of scholars is working on a new edition of Müntzer's works.

[29]Müntzer told Luther in 1524 that he had not been with him "in six or seven years," *MKG* 341:10-11. In his "Confession" of 1525, he also mentioned a stay in Wittenberg in connection with the "Zwickau Prophets," perhaps in 1521/22, Müntzer, (p. 52) suggests a stay of four to five months in 1518. Bubenheimer, "Thomas Müntzer und die Anfänge," 22, is certain that it was "between June/July 1517 and the beginning of January 1519."

Müntzer seems to have been drawn to the new movement through Franz Günther, one of Luther's favorite students, who had been awarded the Biblical Baccalaureate in 1517.[30] Through the efforts of the city magistrate and with the probable help of Luther, Günther received a call to become a "Lutheran" pastor in Jüterbog and became involved in a controversy over Catholic practices with the Franciscans. At Easter of 1519, Günther managed to obtain a position of chaplain (Kaplan) for Müntzer, who immediately became known for his own sermons against the Franciscans.

The Franciscan leader, Bernhard Dappen, complained to the Bishop of Brandenburg that Günther and Müntzer, the disciples of Luther and new sectarians, were exhorting people not to go to confession, not to pray to the saints, not to fast, and to emulate the better Christians, the "Bohemians (Hussites)."[31] Luther heard of the Franciscan's attack and in May of 1519 wrote to the Jüterbog convent in strong defense of Günther and Müntzer. That letter leaves no doubt that Luther acknowledged Müntzer as a faithful companion in the fight against Rome.[32] After the Jüterbog controversy, Müntzer continued his close ties to Luther. He attended the famous Leipzig debate between Luther and John Eck in July 1519 and, perhaps on the basis of another meeting with Luther, accepted an invitation to substitute for Egranus as preacher in Zwickau, a strategic center of the new Lutheran movement.[33] Luther had recommended Müntzer for the position at St. Mary's, while Egranus took a leave of absence—probably because the Zwickau Franciscans had given him a hard time. Egranus was also uncertain regarding his own theological views and, though a "Lutheran," soon aligned himself with the Humanists favoring the old religion.[34]

Müntzer immediately attacked the Franciscans in Zwickau, just as he had done in Jüterbog, and reported his experiences to Luther in a letter dated July

[30]Luther used the occasion for a "Disputation Against Scholastic Theology" and, in ninety-seven theses, asserted that he taught nothing not in agreement with the Catholic church. *Luthers Werke. Kritische Gesamtausgabe* (Weimar, 1833), 1:228.34-36. (Herafter cited as WA.) *Luther's Works* (American Edition, ed. Jaroslav Pelikan and Helmut Lehmann, Philadelphia, 1955-), 31:16. (Herafter cited as LW.) On Günther's background, see Manfred Bensing and Winfried Trillitzsch, "Berhard Dappens 'Articuli . . . Contra Lutheranos.' Zur Auseinandersetzung der Jüterboger Franziskaner mit Thomas Müntzer und Franz Günther 1519," *Zeitschrift für Geschichtswissenschaft* 14 (1967): 115-16.

[31]Ibid., 133. For a solid account of the Jüterbog affair, see Elliger, *Thomas Müntzer*, 53-62.

[32]WA Briefwechsel 1:392.107-115. (Herafter cited as WA BR.) See also below, n104.

[33]There is evidence that Müntzer traveled to Leipzig to buy books. A "shopping list" has survived. See *MKG* 556-60. See also Elliger, *Thomas Müntzer*, 67.

[34]See John Egranus' letter to Luther, dated May 18, 1521: ". . . whom you recommended to me at Leipzig." WA BR 2:346, note a; Elliger, *Thomas Müntzer*, 76. See also Hubert Kirchner, *Johannes Sylvius Egranus* (Berlin, 1961). That Egranus remained an Erasmian humanist has been shown by Georg Buchwald, "Die Lehre des Johann Sylvius Wildnauer Egranus in ihrer Beziehung zur Reformation," *Beiträge zur sächsischen Kirchengeschichte* 4 (1888): 163-202.

13, 1520.[35] Prompted by the Zwickau Council, he also sought Luther's advice regarding the controversy, and included, without commentary, a set of theses drafted by the Franciscan Abbot Tiburtius. These theses accused the "new preachers" (Müntzer and Egranus) of denying essential Catholic doctrines such as the validity of the Mass and the need for meritorious good works. Müntzer addressed Luther as "dearest father (*suavissimus pater*)" whose advice is most welcome. "Whatever you will counsel, I shall do it in the name of the Lord."[36] Müntzer made it quite clear that he and Luther had a common cause against the defenders of the pope, and if Luther and Melanchthon wanted him to continue his attack, he would gladly do so, even though it might lead to suffering. He, Müntzer, felt he had been chosen to engage in other struggles besides the one in Zwickau. Müntzer ended the letter with good wishes for Luther, "you model and torch of the friends of God (*specimen et lucerna amicorum Dei*)" and signed it "Thomas Müntzer, whom you have conceived through the Gospel."[37]

In October of 1520, Müntzer was called to be pastor of St. Catherine's Church in Zwickau, where he continued his attacks against the Franciscans as well as against Egranus, whom he considered a pussyfooting Erasmian Humanist. He drafted twenty-four theses, satirically entitled "Propositions of an Excellent Man Named Ergranus." An inverted reading of them discloses Müntzer's own theological position.[38] Walter Elliger's careful analysis of the Propositions has shown that Müntzer clearly defended Luther's views regarding the centrality of Christ, the correlation of Scripture and Holy Spirit, and the rejection of Humanist rationalism. He remained a "Martinian" in his anti-Catholic stance, but some of his ideas, such as the notion that the Holy Spirit is as powerful a millennium after the apostles as it was in their time (Thesis 22),[39] already hint at his critical distance from Luther. He was also influenced by his reading of the mystic John Tauler (whom Luther praised) and by the charismatic Zwickau leader of a conventicle, Nicholas Storch, who claimed to have "gifts of the Holy Spirit" and favored millennial notions. Nevertheless, he fought the Humanist Egranus on the same basis as he fought the Franciscan Tiburtius: to him they were enemies of the original, apostolic faith that Luther and his movement were trying to restore.[40] Egranus did interpret Müntzer's attack as the work of a Luther disciple: "Your Thomas, as he himself boasts,

[35]*MKG* 13: 357-61.

[36]"Quodcunque suaseris, facturus in domino." *MKG* 359:7-8.

[37]Ibid., 361:8, 10. The last line is not well preserved, but could be reconstructed: "Tomas Munczer qu[an] g[en] u[isti] p[er] evangelium."

[38]Text in *MKG* 513-15. See the excellent treatment by Elliger, *Thomas Müntzer*, 132-66.

[39]*MKG* 515:9-10. Elliger, *Thomas Müntzer*, 164.

[40]Well argued by Elliger, *Thomas Müntzer*, 168.

has come to Zwickau and has confused everything with his crazy mouth and with his doctrines."[41]

Zwickau was soon divided between those who followed Egranus and those who followed Müntzer. When a mob used violence to gain control of the city, Müntzer refused to be a part of it and quietly left town on April 16, 1521, the day of Luther's triumphant entry into Worms. But news reports linked Müntzer to the violence, so Luther withdrew his support, and indeed accused him of satanic practices. "He [Müntzer] and his followers have sown dragons in Zwickau" he told George Spalatin in May of 1522.[42]

From June to November or December of 1521 Müntzer was in Prague. Czech sources depict his stay as a "Lutheran" period. Müntzer had brought along a copy of Melanchthon's theses against scholastic theology, in which he had made a notation describing himself as "an emulator of Martin before the Lord."[43] He was perceived as an excellent representative of Luther's movement and a fine preacher and theologian. One eyewitness recorded that he had heard "Magister Thomas Lutheranus" preach in German and Latin on June 23, 1521.[44] He was received with some pomp and circumstance by the Prague establishment. He preached in the principal churches of the city and he probably lectured at the university.

Müntzer arrived in Prague during a turbulent period for Luther's movement: Luther had been condemned by church and state, and was being concealed at the Wartburg; no strong leader had emerged in Wittenberg to carry on. Did Müntzer go to Prague to unite the old Hussites and the new Lutherans? Did he have ambitions to be the new "Lutheran" leader, based in Prague rather than in Wittenberg? He did, after all, publish the Prague *Manifesto* on All Saints Day, November 1, 1521–Luther had publicized the Ninety-Five Theses on October 31, 1517, the eve of All Saints Day.[45]

None of the four versions of the Prague *Manifesto* mention Luther. They disclose Müntzer who, like John Huss, has experienced spiritual *Anfechtung*; who is ready to die for his cause; and who has been endowed by the Holy Spirit to proclaim "wondrous things" that will be done by God in the Czech lands. The *Manifesto* proclaimed that the climax of divine activity would be a total renewal of the world through the reception of the Holy Spirit, similar to that occurring at the time of the biblical prophets and apostles. In the *Manifesto*

---

[41]Letter to Luther, dated May 1521. WA BR 2:345.16-17.

[42]Dated May 5, 1522. WA BR 2:515.13.

[43]"Emulus Martini apud dominum. . . ." Found not in *MKG*, but in photocopies (*Lichtdrucke*) No. 51 (original in Moscow). See also Elliger, *Thomas Müntzer*, 184.

[44]See Vaclav Husa, *Tomas Müntzer a Cechy* (Prague, 1957), 63. German translation by J. Fanta, "Thomas Müntzer und Böhmen," ibid., pp. 109-21.

[45]This is the oldest version in German. *MKG* 491-94. the other three versions are in *MKG* 495-511. On the history of the texts, see Elliger *Thomas Müntzer*, 188-89.

Müntzer used the language and categories of medieval mysticism to make his point. He complained about the unpastoral and careless attitude of church leaders and he declared his solidarity with the common people as agents of God's will.

In the expanded German version of the *Manifesto*, Müntzer offered an aggressive description of the final renewal at the end of time, his own time: "The time of harvest is now. God has sent me into His harvest. I have sharpened my sickle. . . . He who does not heed the warning will be handed over to the Turks," the final enemy before the coming of the anti-Christ.[46] This German version reveals Müntzer's disappointment with the Prague establishment, which had become suspicious of their German guest and, after vainly urging him to leave, had expelled him from the city in December of 1521.

There is some evidence to show that Müntzer left Prague with a favorable impression of the Taborite faction of the Hussites. In a marginal note in his copy of Tertullian's work on the resurrection, Müntzer noted his disagreement with Tertullian and "the monk Martin Luther" with regard to the second coming of Christ. He apparently agreed with Taborite eschatology, which predicted the imminent end of the world.[47]

After his stay in Prague, Müntzer seemed ready to challenge Luther and the Wittenbergers regarding their theological views. His letter to Philip Melanchthon, dated March 27, 1522, is a case in point. Müntzer begins his letter with the statement that he approves wholeheartedly of the Wittenberg theology because it liberates many souls from the pitfalls of Rome.[48] He chides the Wittenbergers, however, for relying too much on the "dead letter" of Scripture, as exemplified in Luther's insistence that marriage of clergy must be proven from Scripture.[49] Such a narrow view of the Word of God is erroneous, according to Müntzer. "Believe me, God is more willing to speak than you are to hear."[50] He then attempts to persuade Melanchthon of the need to receive the Holy Spirit and thus experience the mystical purification of the soul from worldly emotions: there is need for the "sanctification" of the whole life; such sanctification will create the "elect" who will constitute the future church; and the time is ripe to start such a purified church now. "Our dear Martin acts ignorantly, when he does not want to offend the weak. . . . "[51] According to

---

[46]*MKG* 504:18-19, 35; 505:1.

[47]"Adiungit adventum Antichristi cum die iudicii Sicut Monachus Martinus Luther, ego autem contrarior." This marginal note appears in the copy of Tertullian's treatise on the resurrection (Basel, 1521), 64. R. Schwarz, *Die apokalyptische Theologie Thomas Müntzer*, 2, thinks that Müntzer had turned away from Luther and affirmed Taborite eschatology. But it is difficult to date the marginal note. See Wolfgang Ullmann, "Ordo rerum: Müntzer Randbemerkungen zu Tertullian als Quelle für das Verständnis seiner Theologie," *Theologische Versuche* 7 (1976): 125-40.   [48]*MKG* 380:3-4 (no. 13).

[49]Ibid., 380:9-13.

[50]Ibid., 380:18-19.

[51]Ibid., 381:20-21.

Müntzer, one must act now, and act radically, for hesitation only defeats the cause of renewal. "Dear brother, forego your hesitation, it is time."[52] Since Wittenberg had been experiencing much unrest, and Luther had felt compelled to return from the Wartburg to restore peace through intensive preaching against any radical measures,[53] Müntzer was aware that his statements might arouse negative reactions. He therefore ends the letter with what sounds a little like Luther's declaration at Worms: "you gentle scribes, don't be apprehensive. I cannot do otherwise" and signed it "messenger of Christ (*nuntius Christi*)."[54]

There is evidence to suggest that Müntzer was in touch with Lutherans in Nordhausen and may indeed have been a pastor there for a brief period in 1522.[55] In April of 1522 he also visited his home town of Stolberg. John Spangenberg, the head of the Latin School and a good Lutheran, reported he had heard Müntzer preach a fine sermon which was above criticism.[56] Although he was convinced that the Lutheran movement moved too slowly, Müntzer was apparently eager to maintain contact, and travelled to Wittenberg sometime in April of 1522 to participate in a colloquy with Melanchthon and John Bugenhagen.[57]

The subject of the colloquy is not known, but since Müntzer referred to his visit in connection with the "Zwickau prophets," Nicholas Storch and Marcus Stübner, his relations to them may have been under discussion. In a letter to Luther he stated that, contrary to Luther's opinion, he had had nothing to do with the activities of the "Zwickau Prophets" in Wittenberg. Referring to the severe differences between Paul and the Jewish Christians described in Gal. 2 as an obvious analogy to his own relationship with Storch and Stübner, he wrote, "I do not know what they did, or what they told you."[58]

---

[52]Ibid., 381:23.

[53]Müntzer probably had heard of Luther's famous "Eight Sermons at Wittenberg." WA 10/3:1-64. (*LW* 51:70-100). It can be said that Müntzer detected "an unjustifiable lack of action" (ein unvertretbares Handlungsdefizit) among the Wittenbergers. See Joachim Rogge, "Müntzer und Luthers Verständnis von der Reformation der Kirche" *Thomas Müntzer. Anfragen an die Theologie und Kirche*, 8.

[54]*MKG* 382:2-4. See the analysis of the letter by Schwarz, *Die apokalyptische Theologie Thomas Müntzers*, 35-43, who regards this as the first instance of Müntzer's critical attitude towards Wittenberg.

[55]See Manfred Bensing, "Thomas Müntzer und die Reformationsbewegung in Nordhausen 1522 bis 1525," *Beiträge zur Heimatkunde aus Stadt und Kreis Nordhausen* (Nordhausen, 1983), 4-18, esp. 4-10 on Müntzer's stay in 1522. Bensing links the data to his Marxist views of the peasants' rebellion of 1524/25. Elliger *Thomas Müntzer*, 218-19, has the more balanced view.

[56]Reported by his son, Cyriacus Spangenberg, *Wider die bösen Sieben ins Teufels Karnoffelspiel* (Jena, 1562). Cited by Elliger, *Thomas Müntzer*, 219.

[57]A disciple of Schwenckfeld mentioned the colloquium, Elliger, *Thomas Müntzer*, 228, n60, and Müntzer spoke of a visit to Wittenberg around that time. *MKG* 546:23-24.

[58]"Quid tibi loquuti sint vel quid egerint, ignoro." Letter to Luther, dated July 9, 1523. *MKG* 391:23.

Müntzer's term as pastor of St. John's in Allstedt, from Easter 1523 to August 1524, was marked by attempts to create a model of liturgical reform as he understood it. He began by translating Scripture lessons into German, revising hymns, and revising the traditional services, especially the Sunday Mass.[59] Müntzer, like Luther, was guided by the principle that worship is a matter of cooperation between clergy and laity.[60] He also used Luther's translations, especially the September Bible of 1522, but modified them.

Since Müntzer's entire program of liturgical reform was based on some principles Luther would later use, it is not surprising that he once again tried to make contact with Luther in a letter dated July 9, 1523.[61] Addressing Luther as "most honorable father (*sincerissimus Pater*)," Müntzer began with a declaration of solidarity and a complaint:

> Never has my feeling for your love been so cheap that I would have
> lent an ear to cheap insinuations. For I knew from the very begin-
> ning that you did not plead your own cause but that of all people.
> But I was terribly agitated when you recommended to me in your
> letters this most pestilential Egranus.[62]

This was a reminder that he, Müntzer, saw who Egranus was and what he stood for much better than Luther did. What irked Müntzer particularly was Luther's attempt to reconcile Müntzer and Egranus in order to shield himself from the swarm of his enemies.[63]

Hoping he had cleared the air, Müntzer then went on to explain his position on "revelation," that is, his views of the Holy Spirit, visions, dreams, and their relation to Scripture. The centerpiece of Müntzer's doctrine of revelation is the thesis that true Christianity is based on the testimony of the Holy Spirit in the believer. Only those who "have been taught from the mouth of the living God" know that Christ's teaching is not a human invention but the gift from the living God.[64] Müntzer backed this notion of revelation with references to Scripture, such as Isaiah 8:19ff and John 7:17 which refer to visions

---

[59]*MKG* 15-215. Müntzer's liturgical reforms are analyzed in detail by Elliger, *Thomas Müntzer*, 252-339; for a musicological analysis, see Henning Frederichs in ibid., 339-61. On Müntzer's hymns, see Siegfried Bräuer, "Thomas Müntzers Liedschaffen," *Lutherjahrbuch* 41 (1974): 45-102; on the similarities and differences from Luther's liturgical work, see Karl Honemeyer, *Thomas Müntzer und Martin Luther. Ihr Ringen um die Musik des Gottesdienstes. Untersuchungen zum "Deutzsch Kirchenamt" 1523* (Berlin, 1974).

[60]Elliger, *Thomas Müntzer*, 320, 339 and Honemeyer, *Thomas Müntzer und Martin Luther*, 35-36.

[61]*MKG* no. 40, 389:92.

[62]Ibid., 389:16-20.

[63]Ibid., 389:26-27.

[64]Ibid., 390:10-11.

and recognition of God's word, and stressed dreams and visions as appropriate means of revelation. Aware of Luther's antagonism to such a view—after all, Luther had called such views "satanic" since Müntzer's Zwickau days—Müntzer tried to reassure Luther that he only relied on visions and dreams when they did not contradict the testimony of God's word in Scripture. "Dearest patron," he wrote, "you have come to know Thomas. . . . "[65] In other words, he hoped that Luther knew him well enough not to charge him with teaching strange doctrines; after all, Scripture itself grants validity to prophetic visions and ecstasies. "I am not so arrogant that I would not want to be corrected and taught better by your superior testimony so that we follow the path of love together."[66]

Müntzer mentioned the "Zwickau Prophets," Nicholas Storch and Marcus Stübner, insisting he had nothing in common with them.[67] But he did defend his use of mystical terminology, even though Luther might find it "nauseating." Again he tried to pacify Luther: "Best father, I know that the apostle [Paul] has given me the rule to avoid profane, unusual phrases as well as falsely boasted knowledge. Believe me, I have no intention of saying anything I cannot verify through a clear text of Scripture."[68] He insisted that he, Müntzer, was eager to restore their friendship and to remain in the fellowship of those who lead the movement. "May the Lord protect you and restore the old love," he closed, and added greetings to Melanchthon, Karlstadt, Justus Jonas, and John Agricola.[69]

Luther's response to these assurances was negative. He advised the Allstedt leadership to withdraw its support of Müntzer, and he accused Müntzer of shunning debate and of abusing Scripture.[70]

Müntzer published his views in the treatise *Testimony or Offer of Thomas Müntzer of Stolberg, Pastor in Allstedt, Regarding His Teaching on the Beginning of the Christian Faith and on Baptism.*[71] The treatise was a blast against established Christendom, accusing it of "invented faith" nurtured by hardened hearts, and of a disregard for the biblical testimony of baptism by the Holy Spirit. According to Müntzer, the only alternative is to become "conformed to Christ (*christförmig*)," which means to experience spiritual suffering through the water of doubt and despair—the experience Nicodemus had before he turned

[65]Ibid., 391:7-8.
[66]Ibid., 391:19-21.
[67]Ibid., 391:22-23.
[68]Ibid., 391:25-27.
[69]Ibid., 391:28-392:1.
[70]Letter to George Spalatin, dated August 3, 1523. WA BR 3:120.
[71]*Protestation odder empietung Tome Müntzers, MKG* 225-240. English translation by James M. Stayer, "Thomas Müntzer's Protestation and Imaginary Faith," *The Mennonite Quarterly Review* 55 (1981): 99-130.

to Christ (John 3:5).[72] Without mentioning Luther, Müntzer implied that the new biblical theology was but a continuation of the persistent ecclesiastical sin of clinging to the external word in order to avoid painful spiritual purification through the "inner word," the experiencing of the Holy Spirit. He declared that this subversion of the true faith is embodied in the institution of infant baptism, for which there is no scriptural evidence.[73] He ended the treatise with a call for a more effective reformation based on his own teaching, for he would lead both Protestants and Catholics to a better way:

> I will enhance the doctrine of the evangelical preachers through my undertaking, and also will not disregard our slow Roman brethren. But to put my judgment before the whole world and not into a corner, I sacrifice life and limb for that without any deceitful defense. . . .[74]

Müntzer met with opposition from the Saxon court, which had jurisdiction over Allstedt, but defended his stance in another treatise, *Concerning the Invented Faith*.[75] Once again, Luther and his movement came under Müntzer's theological fire: the authority of the "word" and of the Bible means nothing unless the human heart and soul become transformed by God's Spirit. Holy Scripture is the "dead word" leading anxious consciences into doubt and despair regarding the power of faith.[76] To believe only in the Bible means to have the convenient "sweet Jesus" rather than the "bitter Christ" who purifies the soul. "Those who refuse the bitter Christ will gorge themselves to death with honey."[77] One must die with Christ in order to live with Him; that is, one must truly experience the death of faith in everything creaturely in order to experience true sanctification as one of the "elect" destined to enter the promised new world without sin or death.[78]

Müntzer tried to explain his increasing distance from Luther in these two treatises. He now regarded Luther as the defender of a half-hearted reformation stuck in biblicistic intellectualism which therefore blocked true faith and either an individual or a collective sanctified life. The ever-increasing pressure from the Saxon court, moreover, convinced him that Luther had sold out to

---

[72]*MKG* 222:11, 229:10-13.
[73]Ibid., 228:3-6.
[74]Ibid., 240:2-4.
[75]Ibid., 218-224.
[76]Ibid., 220:22-23.
[77]Ibid., 222:22-23.
[78]Ibid., 224:1-19.

a political Christianity in order to retain his position of leadership.[79] Yet he still hoped to find broad support for his measures designed to correct the Lutheran cause. The people of Allstedt and neighboring communities were flocking to hear his sermons. Müntzer thought it possible that the princes of the land would listen to their people and join his cause. His expectations received a boost when Electoral prince John Frederick and his entourage visited Allstedt to hear his views, which were summarized in July of 1524 in a sermon on Daniel 2 entitled *Sermon to the Princes*.[80]

Müntzer's *Sermon to the Princes* reads like an alternative to Luther's 1523 treatise on temporal authority.[81] Whereas Luther had called for Christian obedience to political authority, Müntzer called on the princes to be obedient to the will of God which demands the separation of the true Christian "elect" from the "godless," by force if need be.

In the sermon, Müntzer belabored the princes to support the movement he, the "new Daniel," would lead in these last days before the end-time. He again attacked Wittenberg. These "inexperienced Bible scholars" merely talk about faith and do not initiate a sanctified life either in themselves or in structures of society.[82] He then reinterpreted Luther's view of political authority (*Obrigkeit*) by asserting that the sword must be used against those who refuse to participate in the reformation of the world through the gospel. "Do not let those who turn us from God live, Deut. 13[:6], for a godless person has no right to live if he impedes the pious."[83] According to Müntzer, such a use of the sword should not be considered sheer violence, but rather the logical consequence of the Word of God that saves the "elect" for their faithful service of preparing the world for the lordship of Christ. Just as the Israelites had taken the land of Canaan, so the princes should form the spearhead for what is to come; the sword is but the means to demonstrate the power of God.[84] Müntzer thus advocated an alliance between himself and the princes, who should, like Nebuchadnezzar, listen to prophetic utterances and so do the will of God.[85]

There is no documentary evidence of any response to the sermon, but Duke Ernst of Mansfield and the other Saxon princes did not like what

[79]Luther and George Spalatin had convinced the Saxon court in Weimar to hold a hearing in which Müntzer was to be asked specific questions by court chaplain Wolfgang Stein. The questions have been preserved: see *MKG* 565. See the detailed account in Elliger, *Thomas Müntzer*, 404-26.

[80]*MKG* 242-63. Elliger, *Thomas Müntzer*, 443-63.

[81]"Temporal Authority: To What Extent It Should Be Obeyed," 1523. WA 11:245-280. (*LW* 45:81-129).

[82]*MKG* 247:18-27.

[83]Ibid., 259:13-15.

[84]Ibid,, 259:28-260:2.

[85]Ibid., 262:5-263:8.

Müntzer was preaching and doing in Allstedt. Müntzer had told Ernst of
Mansfield that, if he should continue to oppose the Allstedt reformation,
Müntzer would deal with him a thousand times worse than Luther had dealt
with the pope.[86] The princes took this threat seriously, since Müntzer had
created a "league of the elect" with paramilitary features in Allstedt. However,
the league did only minor damage to the establishment, such as destroying a
chapel dedicated to the Virgin Mary in the vicinity of Allstedt.

Luther composed his own sermon to the princes in response to Müntzer's,
in which he urged them to silence the "restless spirit."[87] Müntzer responded
by writing to Luther's prince, Elector Frederick the Wise, to complain of
Luther's shameful behavior and to demand freedom of speech even if he did
disagree with Luther.[88]

Concerned about the future, and seemingly frightened, Müntzer fled
Allstedt in August of 1524. But he had used the last weeks in Allstedt to write
another treatise, *An Explicit Exposure of the False Faith of the Unfaithful World*
which was perhaps his first reaction to Luther's scathing attack.[89] Presenting
himself as "Thomas Müntzer with the hammer," he reiterated his view that
"true faith" came through the experiencing of the Holy Spirit, and "invented
faith" was propagated by biblicists. For the first time, Müntzer attacked Luther
head on, calling him "brother soft-living (*Bruder Sanftleben*)" and "father
tiptoe (*Vater Leisentritt*)" who seeks only his own honor instead of the honor
of the gospel.[90] Moreover, he accused Luther of being the "defender of the
godless" because he had asserted it is Christian to obey political authority. He
satirically portrayed the Wittenberg reformer as a willing servant of two
masters—the princes and God—who at the same time accused his opponents of
"enthusiasm (*Schwärmerei*)."[91] To Müntzer, Luther had become the perverted
leader of "usurious evangelists" who bind believers to empty words,[92] which
was why he, Müntzer, had been called by God (through spiritual suffering and
conformity to Christ) to lead people to the "highest faith" through the "over-
shadowing of the Holy Spirit" into a new "holy covenant" begun with
Abraham.[93]

---

[86]Ibid., 394:31-33 (No. 44).

[87]"Letter to the Princes of Saxony Concerning the Rebellious Spirit," 1524. WA 15:210-
221. (*LW* 40:49-59).

[88]August 3, 1524. *MKG* 430-32 (No. 64).

[89]*Ausgetrückte Emplösung des falschen Glaubens*, *MKG* 267-319. On the origins and on the two
versions, see Elliger, *Thomas Müntzer*, 558-66.

[90]*MKG* 282:8-14.

[91]Ibid., 288:26-289:4.

[92]Ibid., 311:21-27.

[93]Ibid., 318:22-37.

The final phase of Müntzer's life, which was tied to the Peasants' War (1524–1525), was increasingly marked by his disappointment about his lack of success in persuading others and by his hatred of Luther, whom he rightly saw as the principal power behind the princes' thrones, intent on preserving religious and political uniformity—either Lutheran or Catholic.

It is in this context that Müntzer wrote and published *A Highly Necessary Defense and Answer Against the Soft-Living Flesh of Wittenberg, Which in Miserable and Perverted Fashion Has Soiled Poor Christendom Through the Theft of Holy Scripture*.[94] Just as Luther had demonized Müntzer, so Müntzer now depicted Luther as an embodiment of Satan: Luther is "the supremely miserly biblicist (*allergeizigster Schriftgelehrter*)," "doctor liar," "doctor of mockery (*doctor ludibrii*)," "the godless Wittenberg flesh," a "deceitful scarecrow" who attacked the "innocent dove" Müntzer, and, indeed, he is Satan himself.[95]

> Sleep well, soft flesh, I'd rather smell you roasting with your insolence through God's wrath, or in a pot over the fire, Jer. 1[:13], than in your own juice, if Satan should devour you, Ez. 23[24:1-13]. You are like donkey meat that would only slowly be done and would be a tough dish for your milkmouths.[96]

Quoting heavily from Scripture, Müntzer once again stated his own position: just as Christ endured suffering and purification, so must every Christian suffer in order to become conformed to Christ. In this sense, Christ and his followers obey the law of God before they are able to experience liberation through the Holy Spirit.[97] Whereas Luther teaches justification "by faith alone," he, Müntzer, is convinced Scripture teaches justification "by the law."[98] Again, Müntzer presented himself as the real pastor of the common people who had been duped by the Wittenbergers into a false faith and who needed to be awakened to the task of preparing themselves for the second coming of Christ.[99] There had been a time when he, Müntzer, had been under the protection of Luther, but only like a lamb is protected by a wolf.[100] Luther had urged the princes to persecute the pastor of Allstedt. But he, Müntzer,

---

[94]*Hoch verursachte Schutzrede und Antwort wider das gaistlosse Sanfftlebende Fleysch zu Wittenberg*, *MKG* 322-43. English trans. Hans J. Hillerbrand, "Thomas Müntzer's Last Tract Against Luther," *Mennonite Quarterly Review* 38 (1964): 20-36. See also Elliger's analysis in *Thomas Müntzer*, 594-626.

[95]*MKG* 323:4-5, 31; 326:25; 327:18-20; 331:27.

[96]Ibid., 341:27-342:2.

[97]Ibid., 324:12-325:21.

[98]Ibid., 330:14-331:14.

[99]Ibid., 335:29-33.

[100]Ibid., 337:13-14.

would, like David, conquer the Goliath Luther.[101] Müntzer ended with a prophecy in both Latin and German:

> O doctor liar, you sly fox, you have saddened the hearts of the righteous with your lies, whom God did not make sad. Thus you have strengthened the power of the godless so that they remained in their old ways; that is why it will happen to you like a fox in a trap: the people will become free and God will be their only Lord.[102]

The Luther Evidence

Müntzer was on Luther's mind from the time of their first encounter in 1518. The Weimar Edition contains about 220 references to Müntzer.[103] Since Luther regarded Müntzer as the *Schwärmer* par excellence, one gets the impression that Müntzer's swarming—whether in ideas or deeds—stung Luther to the degree that he developed an allergy to anything associated with his name.

There is no evidence to suggest that Luther ever actually praised Müntzer, although he did view Müntzer as a supporter of the Reformation in Jüterbog and Zwickau. In a letter dated May 15, 1519, he told the Franciscans in Jüterbog they deserved to be attacked, and asked them to make amends for slandering "him [Müntzer] and us."[104] He counted Müntzer among the "chaplains (*Kaplane*)" who should be called by "Lutheran" congregations, and recommended him to the congregation in Zwickau in 1520.[105] But once Müntzer attacked Egranus in Zwickau, Luther began to consider him "satanic," and never again changed his mind.

It is well known that Luther abhorred any mob action, ranging from mere disrespect for law and order to active revolt against political authorities (*Obrigkeit*). Since some of Müntzer's followers in Zwickau had been involved in political turbulence while he served as pastor there, Luther condemned him as a theological and political hothead who incites violence. Müntzer's strenuous efforts to convince him otherwise were in vain. Luther considered Müntzer's ideas to be the product of a confused and cowardly spirit (*Geist*). "I cannot stand this spirit, whatever he may be. He praises my things but at the

---

[101]Ibid., 342:26-343:3.

[102]Ibid., 343:9-14.

[103]I am grateful to the Tübingen Institute for the Late Middle Ages and the Reformation for supplying me with the "Müntzer" index entries in WA and WA BR. See also Erwin Mühlhaupt, *Luther and Müntzer* (Witten, 1973), listing 106 Luther texts, including references to Müntzer in the correspondence.

[104]Letter to the Franciscan Convent in Jüterbog, dated May 15, 1519. WA BR 1:392.107-115.

[105]Letter from John Egranus to Luther, dated May 18, 1521: "Whom you recommended to me at Leipzig." WA BR 2:346, note a.

same time despises them and aims for something else, something much higher."[106]

Luther also accused Müntzer of ascribing words and phrases to the Bible that were not to be found there, "as if he were mad, or drunk," and of shunning debate.[107] He asked Duke John Frederick of Saxony, in a letter dated June 18, 1524, to use his influence to bring Müntzer to Wittenberg for a hearing. "It is not appropriate that he uses our shadow [sic], our victory, and our advantage—which we gained without his help—against us. It is an evil spirit who sits on our manure and barks at us."[108]

Luther published an open letter to the princes of Saxony, Elector Frederick and Duke John, in July of 1524. The letter, entitled *Letter To the Princes Concerning the Rebellious Spirit*,[109] was Luther's assessment of Müntzer, based on the premise that Satan sends false prophets to oppose the true word of God wherever it is proclaimed. Luther's portrait of Müntzer is more a caricature than a realistic picture based on solid evidence: Müntzer is the "restless spirit" who, like the "unclean spirits" in Matt. 12:43, wanders about trying to find a nest like Allstedt for himself;[110] he is a liar claiming to suffer when no authority has yet prosecuted or persecuted him; he is a part of the "spirit" of the Zwickau Prophets. Since Luther had discovered an inclination towards violence in the Zwickau Prophets, he now asked the princes, as obedient servants of God, to prevent such violence.[111] He added that when Müntzer had visited Wittenberg "once or twice in my cloister, he had his nose punched."[112] Unlike Luther himself, who had humbly faced the threats of Rome at Leipzig and at Worms in debate and had been banned, Müntzer was a boastful spirit unwilling to meet anyone in debate.[113] "I perceive no particular fruit of the Allstedtian spirit except that he wants to use violence and destroy wood and stone."[114] Luther advised the princes to make a distinction between the teaching of false doctrine and the use of physical violence:

> Let them preach against whomever they wish as confidently and boldly as they are able. . . . But when they want to do more than fight with the Word, and begin to use force and to destroy, then your Graces must intervene—whether it be ourselves or they who are guilty—and banish them from the country.[115]

---

[106]Letter to George Spalatin, dated April 3, 1523. WA BR 3:120.28-30.

[107]Ibid., 120:31-32.   [108]WA BR 3:308.73-79.

[109]WA 15:210-221. (*LW* 40:49-71).

[110]WA 15:211.11-14. (*LW* 40:50).

[111]WA 15:212.23-212.3 (*LW* 40:51-52).

[112]WA 15:214.4-5. (*LW* 40:52).

[113]WA 15:215.4-7. (*LW* 40:53-54).   [114]WA 15:217.32-33. (*LW* 40:56).

[115]WA 15:218.19-20; 219.5-7. (*LW* 40:57).

On August 21, 1524, Luther sent a similar letter to the magistrates of Mühlhausen, where Müntzer was now living.[116] He asserted that Müntzer was a wolf in sheep's clothing. The fruits of his spirit were murder and violence, as the people of Zwickau and Allstedt knew, and he and his followers shied away from the light of discussion. According to Luther, their claim is that "Whoever listens to them and follows them is among the elect sons of God; whoever does not listen to them must be godless, and so they wish to kill him"[117]

Rumors regarding the activities of rebellious peasants in Nürnberg and Mühlhausen only confirmed Luther's suspicion that Müntzer was behind it, especially since Müntzer had spent some time in Mühlhausen. "Müntzer is king and emperor in Mühlhausen, not just a teacher."[119]

Luther dealt with the phenomenon of what he considered *Schwärmerei* in the treatise *Against the Heavenly Prophets*, written in the winter of 1524/25. He did allude to Müntzer's attack against "the Soft-Living Flesh in Wittenberg,"[120] but did not mention him by name.

Luther's criterion for judging what is true and what is false teaching is the absolute priority of the external word over against the internal experiencing of the Holy Spirit; the Holy Spirit is bound to the Word. "God has determined to give the inward to no one except through the outward. For He wants to give no one the Spirit or faith outside of the outward word and sign instituted by Him."[121] This order must be carefully observed, Luther contended, because that is the way God reveals Himself. What Luther then said about Karlstadt he could have said about Müntzer: "With all his mouthing of the words, 'Spirit, Spirit, Spirit,' he tears down the bridge, the path, the way, the ladder, all the means by which the Spirit might come to you."[122] To Luther, the issue is the proper relationship between "Word" and "Spirit," and the Word has priority.

> There you have their theology: others are to learn outwardly by their word, which they call an external witness. But they themselves are better and superior to the apostles, and pretend to learn inwardly in their spirit without an external Word and without means, though this possibility was not given to the apostles, but alone to the only Son, Jesus Christ.[123]

[116]WA 15:238-240.   [117]WA 15:239.15-17.

[118]In August and September of 1524. See Elliger, Thomas Müntzer, pp. 568-587.

[119]Letter to Nicholas Amsdorf, dated April 11, 1525. WA BR 3:472.7.

[120]WA 18:86.4. (*LW* 40:107).

[121]WA 18:136.16-18. (*LW* 40:146).

[122]WA 18:137.12-14. (*LW* 40:147).

[123]WA 18:185.21-25. (*LW* 40:195).

In Luther's writings against the rebellious peasants, Müntzer is pointed out as "the arch-devil who rules in Mühlhausen and causes nothing but robbery, murder, and the shedding of blood."[124] Luther was informed of the details of Müntzer's interrogation in prison, and complained about the way it was handled: "He was not asked the right questions; I would have asked quite different ones." But it would not have made any difference, he added, because Satan had hardened Müntzer's heart. "Well, whoever has seen Müntzer may say that he has seen the devil himself in his greatest wrath."[125]

Luther propagated his demonization of Müntzer in the popular treatise of May 1525, *A Terrible Story and Judgment of God About Thomas Müntzer, In Which God Publicly Gives the Lie to This Same Spirit and Condemns Him.*[126] He appealed to the existing climate of superstition in this "report" about the "murderous spirit" by declaring that Müntzer's violent death was a warning to those who still contemplated rebellion; if God had spoken through Müntzer, he would not have ended in the way he did; Müntzer had deserved to die, because he was too boastful about his relationship to God. "Since Thomas Müntzer has failed, it is quite clear that he used God's name but spoke and acted in the name of the devil."[127] Luther ended his "report" with an appeal to the princes to be just in their punishment of the rebels, and merciful to those who repent. He appended copies of the last three letters Müntzer had written during the heat of the rebellion.[128]

Luther continued to refer to Müntzer in various contexts: he told people that his marriage to Catherine von Bora was, among other things, an attestation of the gospel against his enemies like Müntzer and the peasants;[129] in 1526, he boasted of having been the first to detect the real danger of the peasants' rebellion and to block Müntzer's efforts. "He was indeed more against me than against anyone else. It was my head that was most at stake in what the devil planned through him."[130] In sermons, he warned people of the "Müntzerite temptation" to go into a corner to wait for the Holy Spirit instead of trusting the written and spoken Word of God.[131] In 1527, he told his congregation, "Müntzer was among us, but since he wanted to be clever and left us, he became the instigator of the rebellion."[132] In 1528, he told Spalatin

[124]"Against the Robbing and Murdering Hordes of Peasants," 1525. WA 18:357.13-14. (*LW* 46-49).

[125]Letter to John Rühel, dated May 30, 1525. WA BR 3:515.28-516.35.

[126]WA 18:367-374.

[127]WA 18:367.16-17.

[128]WA 18:367.72-372.26. *MKG* 471-474.

[129]Letter to John Briessmann, dated ca. August 15, 1525. WA BR 3:555.13-16.

[130]"Luther's Instruction and Warning Against the Truly Rebellious, Treacherous and Murderous Advice of the Entire Clergy of Mainz," 1526. WA 19:278.23-29.

[131]"Sermons on Exodus," 1524-1527. WA 16:598.12-16.

[132]Sermon of September 16, 1527, on I John. WA 20:674.32-33.

that Müntzer's spirit was still around in Erfurt, where one of the Müntzerites had been inciting rebellion.[133] Luther linked Müntzer to unrest wherever it occurred. "In all these people there is still something of Müntzer's spirit, according to which the godless must be eradicated and the pious should rule the earth.[134]

Luther simplified Müntzer's teachings to make his polemical points: Müntzer denied biblical authority and rejected all externals, he acted without a proper call (*Berufung*), he used his *Anfechtung* to draw attention to himself, he did not distinguish between law and gospel, and he wanted to realize the kingdom of God on earth by means of the sword.[135]

All of Luther's theological polemics were grounded in the notion that Müntzer, under the influence of Satan, had perverted the Lutheran cause. According to Luther, there is a biblical tradition with regard to such perversion: Esau's wives made life bitter for Isaac and Rebeccah (Gen. 26:34-35). Luther asserted that although Müntzer had accused him of starting the gospel but not furthering it, he, Müntzer, had in the end lost his stamina and recanted.[136] He believed that Müntzer was apathetic, unfeeling, an unstable character who could not even find joy in the birth of his son.[137]

In Luther's scheme of history, Müntzer and other heretics are Satan's messengers, sent to keep the church alert in the world. "In short, it is true that wherever God builds a fine, pure church, the devil immediately builds a chapel beside it."[138] Luther still talked about Müntzer as the prototype of all heretics and rebels in his last sermons in 1546. "Heretics and rebels like Müntzer may murmur in the corner, but do not let them go to the pulpit. This is the only way to fight them . . . with the Word and with faith."[139] Even in his very last sermon, on February 15, 1546, he referred to Müntzer as "Master Wiseacre (*Meister Klügling*)" who impeded the gospel's course by trying to dominate it with his own satanic wisdom.[140]

Conclusions

The story of Müntzer's relationship to Luther resembles a Shakespearean tragedy of errors: one hero becomes entangled in a deadly web of circum-

---

[133]Letter dated January 24, 1528. WA BR 4:355.7-8.

[134]Letter to John Hess, dated January 27, 1528. WA BR 4:372.7-8.

[135]Sermon of February 23, 1528. WA 27:56.16-19. Lecture on Isa. 49:3, 1527/29. WA 25:304.19-22. Sermon of February 8, 1540. WA 49:27.17, 29-34. Sermon of January 1, 1532. WA 36:27.33-28.11. Sermons on Matt. 18-24, 1537-1540. WA 47:561.29-42.

[136]Lectures on Genesis, 1535/45. WA 43:496.5-12.

[137]Ibid., WA 44:493.16-26.

[138]Sermon of February 7, 1546. WA 51:175.22-23.

[139]Ibid., WA 51:184.18-24.

[140]Sermon of February 15, 1546. WA 51:188.24; 189.39-190.2.

stances resulting from his utopian sense of mission, ending with his involvement in bloody violence and his death; his opponent defends a questionable tradition of Christian power-plays. Both erred in their judgment of each other, at times each was on the side of the angels. Müntzer's theology of judgment was in error when he called upon the "elect" to slaughter those he deemed "godless"; but he had the sagacity to recognize and expose the sins and heresies of institutionalized Christianity. Luther erred in his pastoral care (*Seelsorge*) when he labeled Müntzer the *Schwärmer* par excellence who can do no right and whose death by violence is proof of divine rejection, but he possessed a Christian realism that preserved him from utopian notions of a Christian life free from earthly struggles against sin, death, and evil. Müntzer tried to realize the impossible dream of creating a world filled with sinless Christians, and died a victim of vengeful Christian political powers.

Luther not only rejected Müntzer the dreamer, he failed to accord him Christian decency and pastoral care. Müntzer was the rejected and condemned prophet without honor in the land he called home. Still, the dramatic story of the Müntzer-Luther encounters yields sufficient evidence to draw some basic conclusions.

1. Müntzer was known as a "Martinian," an "emulator of Martin," and an active participant in Luther's movement of reform until he succeeded in attracting people to his own reform program, particularly during his time as pastor in Allstedt in 1523-1524. Luther had supported Müntzer in his anti-Catholic activities in Jüterbog in 1519 and Zwickau in 1520, until he was informed of Müntzer's connection with what he viewed as sedition. Müntzer's correspondence with Luther and Melanchthon clearly demonstrates that he tried to maintain contact with them, if only to persuade them that he was a better reformer than they.

But it cannot be demonstrated that Müntzer's early views regarding God, salvation, and the world were decisively shaped by Luther, despite their meeting in 1518. It is also difficult to show when Müntzer became attracted to mystical ideas or to the *devotio moderna* and to the spiritual burdens of lay people.[141] One could surmise that Luther's endorsement of John Tauler, whom he regarded as the author of the *Theologica Germanica*, which he edited in 1518, introduced Müntzer to German mysticism. A nun named Ursula once chided Müntzer in 1520 for being too deeply immersed in his reading of Tauler and Henry Suso to care about life around him.[142] He certainly seemed

---

[141]Attempts have been made to see such influences in Müntzer's stay in Braunschweig. See Bräuer, "Thomas Müntzers Beziehungen zur Braunschweiger Frühreformation," 637. However, the sources are too scanty.

[142]*MKG* no. 11, 356:16-18.

to be "a bookworm in a nunnery" at that time,[143] and he may have hoped to persuade Luther by these means to join him in his "radical reformation." But in 1521, when Luther increased his attacks on Müntzer and urged the Saxon princes to move against "the restless spirit of Allstedt," Müntzer finally broke with him and relied instead on what he perceived to be a new age initiated by the peasants' rebellion in 1524/25.

2. Though fragmentary, Müntzer's literary legacy discloses a religious and theological development culminating in the preaching of a biblical gospel radically different from Luther's version of the Word of God. Müntzer was driven "from earliest years (*von Jugend auf*)" by the desire to attain "the invincible faith" promised to Christians.[144] But he could not attain that faith through the established Christendom that Rome and Wittenberg represented, since both claimed that faith comes through trust in the institutional church and/or in the external word expounded by intellectuals versed in Scripture. After searching through Scripture and tradition—especially prophets, apostles, and the Ante-Nicene fathers including the church historians Eusebius and Hegesippus—Müntzer discovered the simple truth stated by Paul and other early Christians that "human hearts are the paper on which God writes with His finger His immovable will and eternal wisdom" (II Cor. 3:3); and that anyone with an open mind can have such a heart and thus receive the living Spirit of God.[145]

Describing the subjective experiencing of the Holy Spirit in mystical categories, Müntzer attempted to develop a theology of history centered in the notion that a cadre of Spirit-filled members of a "league of the elect," charged with finding the final solution to the problem of evil, would restore fallen creation in the final phase of history.[146] According to Müntzer, the elect would

---

[143]See Gritsch, *Reformer Without a Church*, 13-18. Even Goertz, who contends that Müntzer was a mystic, concedes that he was his own man with his own theological and political agenda. See above, n20. Whether the young Luther was decisively shaped by German mysticism is also questionable. For a defense of this position, see Bengt R. Hoffman, *Luther and the Mystics. A Re-Examination of Luther's Spiritual Experience and His Relationship to the Mystics* (Minneapolis: Augsburg, 1976), esp. 217-36. For a rejection of that view, see Lohse, "Luther und Müntzer," 17. Luther cannot be viewed as a mystic since he always stressed the external word.

[144]First version of the *Prague Manifesto*, MKG 491:3.

[145]Ibid., 492:7-8. This emphasis on the Holy Spirit created the tension with regard to Luther's emphasis on the Word. Müntzer's theology and piety cannot be understood unless this tension is taken into consideration. See also Joachim Rogge, "Wort und Geist bei Thomas Müntzer," *Die Zeichen der Zeit* 29 (1975): 137.

[146]Müntzer's theology of history has been traced to the Old Testament. See Abraham Friesen, "Thomas Müntzer and the Old Testament," *Mennonite Quarterly Review* 47 (1973): 5-19. Friesen even saw connections with Joachim of Fiore's notion of three kingdoms. Ibid., 17-18. See also Rolf Dismer, "Geschichte, Glaube, Revolution. Zur Schriftauslegung Thomas Müntzer" (Hamburg Dissertation, 1974). Müntzer's use of the Old Testament has also been linked to his work with patristic sources. See Wolfgang Ullmann, "Das Geschichtsverständnis Thomas Müntzers," *Thomas Müntzer. Anfragen an die Theologie und Kirche*, 50-51.

first try to persuade the rulers of the world to cooperate with the will of God revealed to individual prophets like himself and his comrades; if the rulers' hearts remained hardened, their subjects would rise in revolt against them and thus execute the divine plan. Müntzer's tragic error was to see global Armageddon in such an insignificant event as the peasants' rebellion, and, with a total lack of military common sense, to urge Saxon peasants to revolt.

3. Luther may have had an early interest in applying the gospel of God's free and justifying grace to socio-political structures.[147] Nevertheless, he remained a defender of the Corpus Christianum and rejected as *schwärmerisch* any notion of theocracy in the sense of a transformation of the world through Spirit-filled mob action such as Müntzer advocated. He also developed a view of history which portrayed *Schwärmer* like Müntzer, Sacramentarians, Papists, Jews, and Turks as Satan's "fifth column."

When challenged by the *Schwärmer* in his own camp, Luther confronted them with a prophetic authority which he regarded as "right" compared to their perverted prophesies. In his eyes, they were the "false brethren" who had become disciples of Satan and, by their resistance to his gospel, had disclosed their truly satanic nature. As a result, Luther maligned these "false brethren," arguing that he himself was on the side of God, for, even though He still hid behind the mask of history,[148] God had left sufficient scriptural clues to a proper theological understanding of the relationship between His Holy Spirit—linked to the eternal Word—and the world, His creation.

According to Luther, the principal issue in Müntzer's *Schwärmerei* was Müntzer's confusion of God's judgment, His law, with God's mercy, His gospel—a confusion already apparent in his insistence that Christians must use the law of Moses to create a new world devoid of the sin revealed n the Mosaic law. Müntzer had justified the destruction of images and of the Mallerbach chapel by the "league of the elect" by claiming that this was the application of the Mosaic law which was fulfilled in Christ. According to Luther, such a claim transformed Christ's gospel into a legalistic mandate,[149] and this confusion of law and gospel was nothing but the most visible work of Satan.

---

[147]Some Luther interpreters have tried to show that Luther's treatise "To the Christian Nobility" aims at socio-political reform, as is indicated by the subtitle "Concerning the reform of the Christian estate." But there is more evidence to support Luther's defense of Constantinian Christendom than supporting a program of social and political reform. See Günter Mühlpfordt, "Der frühe Luther als Autorität der Radikalen. Zum Luther-Erbe des linken Flügels" in *Weltwirkung und Reformation. Referate und Diskussionen*, ed. Max Steinmetz and Gerhard Brendler, 2 vols. (Berlin, 1969), 213. See also Grane's critique, "Thomas Müntzer und Martin Luther," 8.

[148]On Luther's view of history in relatin to the *Schwärmer*, especially to Luther and Müntzer and Karlstadt, see Mark U. Edwards, *Luther and the False Brethren* (Stanford, Calif.: Stanford University Press, 1975), 199-205.

[149]Müntzer advocated such a fusion of law and gospel in his "Sermon to the Princes," 1524: those who have experienced the Holy Spirit must destroy the altars of the godless and subdue them (Deut. 7:5-6). This is the fulfillment of the law in the gospel of Christ (Matt. 5:17). *MKG* 260:13-17.

4. Müntzer's quest for personal religious certainty had led him to study the pluriformity of the Christian tradition and to focus on what could be called the "cosmic Christology" of the ante-Nicene Fathers, who were concerned for the restoration of God's fallen creation through the work of Christ. Müntzer described Christ's cosmic work of restoration in strongly mystical categories borrowed from German mystics like John Tauler, the powerful preacher of the late Middle Ages. It may have been from the German that Müntzer learned to speak of "faith" as "infused" (*fides infusa*)—a prevalent notion in medieval mysticism that thought of faith in material, and indeed physical, "realistic" terms, over against the "conceptualist" tradition linked to Neoplatonic thought. Müntzer saw Christ's cosmic work begin in the "depth of the soul" of the believers who, as the "elect" of God, would apply their internal experiencing of the purifying Holy Spirit to the external structures of the world.

Given Müntzer's theological perspective, he could never really understand Luther's exposition of the Word of God as the center of a theology of the cross that proclaimed God's non-metaphysical revelation embodied in the historical Jesus of Israel. He also misunderstood Luther's linking of the Holy Spirit to the proclaimed, written, and sacramentally enacted Word, for he called it the subjective speculation of a biblicistic intellectual. To Müntzer, the Holy Spirit is the time-transcending power that links him, Müntzer, to the biblical prophets and apostles and therefore grants him the same authority they had claimed. It is this kind of "spiritualism" that propelled Müntzer to, if not beyond, the periphery of mainstream Christian tradition which claims to be bound to both the authority of Scripture and the dogma of the Trinity.

Luther quickly detected this "heresy" and warned against it for the rest of his life. Although he seemed quite capable of exercising patient pastoral care in certain situations, he was apparently incapable of linking his theological sagacity to stamina in pastoral care and fair debate when it came to Müntzer. His own preoccupation with the work of the devil fed his impatience towards Müntzer and those he deemed Müntzer's followers, and resulted in polemics marked by subjectivist judgments and speculations.[150]

Müntzer's radical sense of solidarity with those who, in his judgment, endured the most severe *Anfechtung* and who were saved from spiritual death through the miraculous intervention of the Holy Spirit, serves as a reminder and an admonition to any church in any age to see the gospel as a divine power

---

[150]See, for example, Luther's speculations about the chronology of world history in his *Supputatio annorum mundi*, in which he presents the scheme of seven millennia. WA 53:22. See also John M. Headley, *Luther's View of Church History* (New Haven: Yale University Press, 1963), ch. 3. Luther's subjectivistic speculations about the will of the hidden God are evident in his anti-Jewish writings, especially "Against the Sabbatarians," 1538. WA 50:336.2-6. (*LW* 47:96). See also Eric W. Gritsch, *Martin—God's Court Jester. Luther in Retrospect* (Philadelphia: Fortress Press, 1983), 99-103 on the history and ch. 7 on Luther and the Jews.

having socio-political implications.[151] It seems ironic that while Luther was condemning Müntzer as a satanic prophet creating chaos in the Corpus Christianum, Müntzer was proclaiming his commitment to restoring the divine order of the original creation.

Luther considered Müntzer merely a satanic prophet advocating sedition and violence. After Luther urged the Christian political establishment to counteract the Müntzerite "heresy," Müntzer saw Luther as the satanic defender of the status quo. They thus reduced each other to convenient targets for demonization, and that is the real tragedy of errors. Those who live after them need to find a better way to quarrel about the truth of the gospel.

[151]Lohse, "Luther und Müntzer," 32.

"Brushwood Sermons" near Antwerp
Engraving by Franz Hogenberg, 1566

Lay Preaching and Radicalism
in the Early Reformation

Siegfried Hoyer

THAT THE SERMON WAS THE PRIMARY MEDIUM OF EXPRESSION for the Reformation is a commonplace observation of Reformation historians. But what is conspicuous for the church historian is that this was not just a simple occurrence, but that it also coincided with the fundamental elements of the self-understanding of the early Reformation. The claim was made for a new, authoritative interpretation of the Bible and so it became in theological terms the proclamation of the Word of God; the sermon was the ultimately decisive event. The sermon was like a means of grace, and as such it partially displaced the means of grace of the medieval church, the sacraments. Thus the sermon assumed a unique role in theology and a significance which it had never before assumed in the history of the church."[1] Comments similar to this can be found in many studies and have become part of our general understanding of the Reformation.

In contrast stands the complicated task of reconstructing the content of lay sermons from the primary sources and the equally difficult task of discovering the origin and previous occupation of the new preachers.[2] While the visitations, which marked, when they began in 1526, the beginning of the institutionalization of the new church, tell us much about the evangelical pastors of that time,[3] we have only scattered and often only vague information about the preceding ten years, during which the many currents of reform were first united in a broad anti-Roman Catholic movement which subsequently splintered as the social and revolutionary demands of the common man reached their culmination.

Can the analysis of the configuration of the Reformation preachers obtained from visitation records be applied retrospectively to the first decade

---

[1]Bernd Moeller, "Einige Bemerkungen zum Thema Predigten in reformatorischen Flugschriften," in *Flugschriften als Massenmedien der Reformationszeit*, ed. Hans-Joachim Köhler (Stuttgart, 1981), 263.

[2]Bernd Moeller, "Was wurde in der Frühzeit der Reformation in den deutschen Städten gepredigt?" *Archiv für Reformationsgeschichte* 75 (1984): 176ff.

[3]These and the parish books introduced in different Lutheran regions provide the material for the study of Susan C. Karant-Nunn, "Luther's Pastors: the Reformation in the Ernestine Countryside," *Transactions of the American Philosophical Society* 69 (1979): 8; Bernhard Klaus, "Soziale Herkunft und theologische Bildung lutherischer Pfarrer in der reformatorischen Frühzeit," *Zeitschrift für Kirchengeschichte* 80 (1969): 22ff.; Martin Brecht, "Herkunft und Bildung der protestantischen Geistlichen des Herzogtum Württemberg im 16. Jh.," ibid., 163ff.

of the Reformation? Partially due to the influence of Humanism, laymen were afforded high respect in many pamphlets. In view of this, what opportunities to preach were open to them? It was Luther who had suggested to Cochläus that a layman, or more precisely a boy of eight or nine years of age, might act as judge in a religious dispute,[4] and as early as 1520, in his pamphlet *To the Christian Nobility*, Luther identified all Christians as clergy and suggested that the only distinction should be that of office. We will return to Luther's sweeping assertion that a shoemaker, blacksmith, peasant, indeed, anyone who carried on a trade was equal to an ordained priest and a Bishop.[5]

The study of the impact of lay preachers in the early Reformation calls for a precise definition of laity. In the Middle Ages, the meaning of "laity" included all non-ordained Christians. While the New Testament recognized the authority of all believers to preach, it is generally accepted that a division began to develop as early as the third century when particularly gifted men were called out of the ordinary ranks and ordained as clergy. This division was eventually formalized in canon law,[6] restricting the authority to administer the sacraments, including the authority to preach, to ordained priests. The fifth century brought the *statuta ecclesiae antiqua* which reserved the authority to teach and preach to priests,[7] excluding both laymen and non-ordained monks, of whom there were large numbers in the various monastic orders of the late Middle Ages. It must therefore be emphasized that the distinctive emphasis in the following examples falls upon ordination, not education. The essential attribute of a priest at that time was ordination, not education. Once this essential attribute of the priesthood had been formally established by the process just described, the laity were left only with the privilege of receiving the means of grace administered by the church.

To this position of the church on lay preaching evolved by the fifth century, there were, of course, exceptions. These existed throughout the system, were officially sanctioned, but were of little consequence compared with the radical break practiced in the heretical communities of the Waldensians, *Humiliati*, Taborites, and others. But even most of these groups soon developed a strong tendency away from the altogether free proclamation of the Word and moved toward establishing their own forms of priesthood or clergy.

The term "Early Reformation" is vague, and the following considerations were taken into account for establishing a precise time frame for this essay. The suppression of the peasants' uprising and the beginning of the Anabaptist movement in 1525 and 1526 had a radical bearing on our topic, especially

[4]Helmar Junghans, "Der Laie als Richter im Glaubensstreit der Reformationszeit," in *Luther-Jahrbuch* 39 (1972): 31ff.

[5]WA 6:401, 409.

[6]H. E. Feine, *Kirchliche Rechtsgeschichte*, 3d ed. (Weimar, 1955), 1: 47ff., 379.

[7]Yves Congar, *Der Laie. Entwurf einer Theologie des Laientums*(Stuttgart, 1956), 498.

with respect to the response of the authorities to these events, Luther's attitude toward preaching (of which more will be said presently), and the involvement of the laity in the exposition of the Bible. I will, therefore, draw the dividing line approximately in 1526 so that the two years of the peasants' uprising are included in our analysis. In external agreement with this line of demarcation is the Regensburg Convention of June 6, 1524 which tightened the regulations governing the education of priests. This was clearly a step against anyone preaching without ordination. From the reformers' side, Eberlin von Günzburg commented with the prophecy that "now even the peasants will appoint clergy.[8]

Before reviewing extant lay sermons and their related heuristic and substantive issues, it should be noted that we need to consider the response and the scope given to lay preaching by church institutions and secular authorities as well as by Luther, Karlstadt, Müntzer, and Zwingli, who may be said to represent the various currents of the Reformation. Finally, at least an attempt should be made to establish the content of lay sermons from the scarce information at our disposal. Where did they fall in the broad spectrum of Reformation preaching which stretches from Luther to Müntzer? Were these sermons initially more or less radical than those of the clerics who had sided with the Reformation? We need to keep in mind that even though this study is limited to preaching, a clear separation between the sermon and the pamphlet is not possible. Many, though, of course, not all sermons were printed, which brought a number of restrictions into play. On the other hand, pamphlets or parts of pamphlets were read publicly, even in churches, and thus virtually became sermons in function.

In compliance with canon law, Roman Catholic clergy, together with the municipal and regional authorities who remained loyal to the old church, such as Duke George of Saxony, consistently and radically interfered with any lay efforts to preach. But far more remarkable than the response of the rulers was the mobility of the laymen who challenged them. Municipal authorities, who favored the reformers but had followers of the old church still sitting on town councils, behaved inconsistently. Luther's position on lay preaching was not the least significant cause of this diversity.[9]

During the early years of the Reformation, until about 1522/23, Luther expressed himself on the subjects of laity, faith, and preaching in widely varying contexts, and so we must extract his opinion from diverse references. His emphasis on the priesthood of all believers and the equal status which he accords to shoemakers, blacksmiths, peasants, and priests in *To the Christian Nobility* might lead one to believe that Luther understood the concept of the

---

[8]Justus Maurer, *Prediger im Bauernkrieg* (Stuttgart, 1979), 36.

[9]M. Doerne, "Predigtamt und Prediger bei Luther," in *Wort und Gemeinde: Festschrift für Erdmann Schott* (Berlin 1967), 46ff.; E. Winkler, "Luther als Seelsorger und Prediger," in *Leben und Werk Martin Luthers 1526-1546*, ed. Helmar Junghans (Berlin, 1983), 233 ff.

priesthood of all believers to mean that the laity had the same authority as had the priests in every facet of the proclamation of the faith. Such a generalization is, however, erroneous. Luther placed distinct limitations on the laity when he observed elsewhere that the only difference between laymen, priests, princes, bishops, religious and secular, was one of "office and calling" since they are all clergy.[10] One cannot fail to see the qualification he made here with regard to different callings and offices. On the other hand, the reference to the office is not yet as strong as it is in 1531 when Luther stated that anyone preaching must be properly appointed.

Luther came closest to addressing the topic directly in 1523 when he wrote about the right and authority of a Christian congregation to judge all doctrine and to appoint and recall teachers (*Daß eine christliche Versammlung oder Gemeine Recht und Macht habe all Lehre zu urteilen und Lehrer zu berufen, ein- und abzusetzen*).[11] This was not a matter to be governed by man-made laws, customs, traditions, etc., and all teachers (i.e. preachers) and their doctrine had to be subjected to the judgment of the congregation. The congregation was to appoint its preachers, those who had the calling and had been enlightened and endowed by God. It was not merely a Christian's right and capacity to spread the Word of God, but also his duty.[12]

To understand Luther's intention one must take a close look at these sentences. At first glance they would seem to give all Christians complete freedom to preach. Luther elaborated the notion by answering the question whether a Christian may preach if he has not been appointed. The answer is that he may do so without special appointment in a place where there are no Christians. In the presence of Christians, however, he should be called from among their midst except in cases where there is a lack of teachers.[13] A layman may indeed become a preacher but should secure an appointment from the congregation. In 1523 Luther advised the City Council of Prague concerning such appointments in his tract *De instituendis ministris ecclesiae* and even dealt with the formalities of the procedure.[14] In the first half of the 1520s Luther thought that the congregation was capable of deciding on the proper manner of preaching the gospel, and this notion was followed by a number of municipal magistrates during the early years of the Reformation.

There is, nonetheless, a clear reference to the office of preaching in Luther's words, when he gives the congregation the right of appointment and examination. Anyone wishing to preach should seek an appointment (a requirement initially limited to normal circumstances). Preaching as an office

[10]WA 6:408.
[11]WA 34: 1:136ff., 422ff.
[12]WA 11:408ff.
[13]WA 11:412.
[14]WA 12:169ff.

demanded not only special talents but also public confirmation. Luther himself practiced what he preached and wrote. Georg Rörer, a Master of Arts enrolled at the University of Wittenberg in 1522, was shortly thereafter given the position of deacon of the town church. After a purely academic career he lacked confirmation as a priest and received it personally from Luther on May 15, 1525.[15] Rörer is one of a comparatively large number of university graduates who became evangelical preachers.

Luther had a completely negative attitude regarding women preaching, of which a few instances had been reported to him from Thuringia and Saxony. He expressed himself in very plain terms in a table talk from the early 1530s: "Women are experts at household affairs and can talk about them in sweet and lovely voices surpassing even Cicero, the most eloquent of orators . . . but when they leave the household to speak about public affairs nothing much comes of it. For even though they may have words aplenty, they lack expertise and understanding, which makes them talk silly and confused nonsense."[16]

This was in stark contrast to the position of Karlstadt whose respect for the laity made him come to completely different conclusions. Both agreed, however, on the universal priesthood of all believers, with the difference that Karlstadt opposed the formal appointment of preachers and ministers.[17] Preaching required a special inner awakening and a calling which must come from God. He once wrote to the congregation at Orlamünde: "What would you say to the proposition that no one should write or preach or perform a public function on God's behalf without being elected to it by Him?"[18] The congregation has the task of testing the preacher and ascertaining his divine vocation.

The spiritualist element evident here brought Karlstadt close to Müntzer's position, but it also made preaching possible for a number of laymen who felt the call of God. There can be no doubt that several followed this spiritual lead.

In the case of Müntzer, the decisive change of mind concerning lay preaching came when, while working at St. Catherine's Church, he met the cloth makers and journeymen from Zwickau. Whether it was brought about by the deep impression left on Müntzer by the piety of the laymen of the circle of Storch, the so-called "Secta Storchitarum," or possibly by a lay interpretation of the Bible, is open to speculation. Public preaching by Storch and his followers would have been an exception before the middle of 1521 as such an

---

[15]Bernhard Klaus, "Georg Rörer, ein bayrischer Mitarbeiter D. Martin Luthers," *Zeitschrift für bayrische Kirchengeschichte* 26 (1957): 115ff.

[16]WA TR 1: no. 1084. On the subject of women preachers see also TR 3: no. 3813 and 6: no. 6567.

[17]Hermann Barge, *Andreas Bodenstein von Karlstadt* (Leipzig, 1905), 81; Calvin A. Pater, *Karlstadt as the Father of the Baptist Movement* (Toronto: Toronto Universtiy Press, 1984), 66ff.

[18]Andreas Karlstadt, *Schriften aus den Jahren 1523-1525*, vol. 1, ed. E. Hertsch (Halle, 1956).

activity could not have occurred on a large scale under the eyes of the town council and the Elector's representative. When it later caused an uproar, Müntzer had long been expelled from the town.[19] For an account of what happened during his presence, probably in the first few months of 1521, we can refer to a satirical poem from Egranus's circle. At that time, Müntzer himself had not yet spoken out on the role of the laity in spreading the gospel, and when he did so later, he restricted himself to using the abstract theological term "the elect." The "elect" person, said Müntzer, may be a layman but does not have to be one. A poem from the spring of 1521 accused him of "preferring journeymen, and particularly one Nickel Storch, whose praises he sang from the pulpit and whom he elevated over all priests." Storch had even taken to street corner preaching, charged the poem, and named Picardy as an example. In the end, Müntzer is said to have "sanctioned this Nickel Storch . . . from the pulpit, and now laymen will become our prelates and ministers and give account of the faith."[20]

These lines suggest that Müntzer not only promoted lay preaching, but also publicly proclaimed it as an alternative to the work of ordained priests. By initiating and supporting it from the pulpit, he went farther than any of the other reformers whose views are presented here. His respect for the laity did not, however, become part of his theology in subsequent years.

As we noted at the beginning, the main reason for limiting our information on non-ordained preachers is the scarcity of extant sources. Only in a few cases do we know the content of the sermons and whether they drew on Luther's basic position or represented a more radical position. In the latter case, we would want to know what issues were raised, which theological or social questions, including the issue of obedience to ecclesiastical and secular authorities. Furthermore, it is evident that the material which found its way into print represents a weighted selection emphasizing *non-radical* pieces since even Karlstadt's writings, which appeared between 1522 and 1525, not to mention the works of Müntzer, were criticized and suppressed in cities which had evangelical councils such as Nuremberg and Basel. In the brief notices that have come down to us, often from orthodox Catholic chroniclers, we find terms such as "radical" and "inflammatory" of which we must be particularly wary. In this connection, Thomas Murner's remark in his polemical tract *Concerning the Great Lutheran Fool* comes to mind that "Luther's doctrine is a Bundschuh."[21]

Regions and towns that remained Catholic began immediately to persecute lay preachers. The local rulers and magistrates were not only strictly

---

[19]Siegfried Hoyer, "Die Zwickauer Storchianer–Vorläufer der Täufer?" *Jahrbuch für Regionalgeschichte* 13 (1985): 68ff.

[20]J. K. Seidemann, *Thomas Müntzer: Eine Biografie* (Dresden, 1842), 110.

[21]Th. Murner, *Deutsche Schriften*, vol. 9 (Straßburg 1918), 104, "das Luthers ler ein buntschuh."

opposed to any violation, but also responded with the expulsion or even execution of offenders. The problems connected with lay preaching are well illustrated by events reported from Delitzsch (in the Duchy of Saxony) and the story of the person called Karsthans.

On September 1, 1522 the parish priest at Delitzsch complained to his ruler that the schoolmaster Johann Zymler had addressed a sizable crowd speaking from the school building, directing his words toward the churchyard. He "brought shame and disgrace on our priests and myself."[22] Duke George of Saxony responded the same day by instructing the town council to imprison the schoolmaster who, as a layman, had no right to preach. When the council reported that the order had been carried out four days later, an apology from Zymler was attached. It stated that he had had no intention to preach "but to hold a disputation from the school window, and there was no one present. . . ."[23] Zymler thus extricated himself from his difficulty with relative ease.

A similar story is that of Karsthans whose name was Hans Maurer. He was also known by the name of Zündauf and practiced medicine, apparently without a diploma from a faculty of medicine.[24] Karsthans first preached in Strasbourg, then in Freiburg and later in Balingen, probably following Luther's basic lines of argument. But during his time in Strasbourg, we know of radical statements directed against the clergy and a call for their abolition. He was arrested by the Habsburg authorities in Württemberg, was transferred to Tübingen, and was interrogated there under torture. Then we lose track of him. Both Karsthans and Zymler had academic backgrounds, and even though they were laymen, they were not uneducated.

Belonging to the same social group was Georg Mohr who also preached from a school window but in a town that had become largely evangelical, namely Wittenberg. His biographer Sebastian Fröschel tells us that Mohr preached because of a general discontent with the system of university studies. The activist schoolmaster enjoyed the support of a prominent circle, including Melanchthon, Spalatin, and others at Wittenberg and in subsequent years we find him as an ordained cleric in Coburg, then at Borna, later at Naumburg cathedral, and finally as superintendent at Torgau. As a layman, he proceeded along the path laid out by Luther in 1523 by seeking ordination or obtaining appointment as a minister, without the normally required specialized education.[25]

[22]F. Gess, ed., *Akten und Briefe zur Kirchenpolitik Herzog Georgs von Sachsen*, (Leipzig, 1905), 1: 348.

[23]Ibid., 355.

[24]Josef Fuchs, in *Neue Deutsche Biographie*, (Berlin, 1977), s.v. 'Karstans.'

[25]Otto Clemen, "Der Bauer von Wöhrd," *Beiträge zur Reformationsgeschichte aus Büchern und Handschriften der Zwickauer Ratsschulbibliothek*, (Berlin, 1902), 2: 25ff.

A relatively large percentage of lay preachers held the degrees of Master or Bachelor of Arts and were former teachers in elementary or municipal grammar schools. Several examples show that some of the new evangelical preachers came from this group. Statistics compiled by Susan Karant-Nunn listing ordinations at Wittenberg show that there were about 20 percent teachers among the new preachers for each year from 1537 onwards.[26]

One example was Johann Agricola from Eisleben. In 1514 he was a teacher at Braunschweig, where he became a friend of Müntzer, but later attacked him in several pamphlets. Even though he rose to the position of preacher at the cathedral and superintendent in Brandenburg after 1540, Agricola was never ordained as a minister.[27] This illustrates that despite Luther's insistence upon ordination there were isolated cases where this was not implemented. It might be worth noting that Luther, in a table talk in 1540, remarked that no preacher should be chosen who had not taught school.[28]

A number of lay preachers in various regions were explicitly nominated by the congregation, possibly in preference to other candidates, and in defiance of objections from the authorities. In some cases the motive may have been a shortage of suitable ministers.[29] While we have no reports on the content of their sermons, we may assume that they more or less adhered to the positions advocated by Luther. The revolutionary peasants made their own choice at times. An account of the rebellion at Ohrdruf in Thuringia states that in 1525 the insurgents wished to make Philip, a miner, their preacher.[30] This they promptly did, and the sources even mention the stipend he was paid. Philip evidently was a talented speaker, and the peasants bluntly turned down the preacher nominated by evangelical town council of Ohrdruf. We may assume that Philip's sermons were radical and that he identified with the social and revolutionary demands of the peasants. There are also instances in the Swiss Confederation where pressure was applied by communities to keep the preacher of their choice. When a layman entered the church at Eglisau in 1521/22, the sexton sought to deny him access to the pulpit and a wrestling match ensued. It was then that a member of the congregation shouted at the priest: "You will let him preach because the church is ours and not yours."[31]

[26]Karant-Nunn, "Luther's Pastors," 10ff.; Klaus, "Soziale Herkunft," 44.

[27]G. Kawerau, *Johann Agricola aus Eisleben* (Berlin, 1881), 32.

[28]Luther, WA TR 5: no. 5232.

[29]As happened in Neustadt/Orla in 1522/23 (K. Herrmann, *Die Einführung der Reformation in Neustadt,* [1927], 13ff.) and in Kamenz where the former town judge became a preacher; F. Ronneberger, "Eine Kamenzer Kirchenordnung," *Beiträge zur Sächsischen Kirchengeschichte* 27 (1914): 218ff.

[30]Walther P. Fuchs, ed., *Akten zur Geschichte des Bauernkrieges in Mitteldeutschland,* (Jena, 1942), 2: 429ff.

[31]Emil Egli, ed., *Aktensammlung zur Geschichte der Zürcher Reformation in den Jahren 1519-32,* reprint ed., (Nieuwkoop, 1973), 106.

This affirmed the congregation's right to choose its own preacher, a demand contained in the first of the Twelve Articles drawn up by the rebellious peasants in 1525. Radical preaching must be assumed in this case.

Women preachers caused a particular sensation, not only because women, just as laity in general, had been excluded from the priestly office in the medieval church, but also because Luther's initially indifferent view later turned into outright opposition. Probably the most interesting instance occurred in the circle of the *Secta Storchitarum* in Zwickau.

In July 1521, a few months after Müntzer's expulsion from the town, the local authorities were driven into a frenzy of activity because women had dared to preach "from the pulpit."[32] This must be viewed against the particular social background in which women played a special role. Zwickau's main industry was clothmaking and there were a number of women among the journeymen. We may assume that their social position was as depressed as that of their male colleagues, but business was thriving at the time and under these conditions women clothmakers were an indispensable part of economic life.

Duke John, the local ruler, was well disposed toward the Reformation by 1521; whether he was offended by the women is an open question. But the events caused such a stir that the vicar general for Zeitz/Naumburg promptly intervened on behalf of the bishop and Nikolaus Hausmann, the new preacher at Zwickau, was called upon to report to the Elector. This public preaching by women prompted the authorities to investigate the lay circle around Nikolaus Storch, an action which led to a hearing in December 1521. It may be assumed that the women preachers propagated the same radical theological views of the *Secta Storchitarum* as Storch, Drechler and Stübner propagated in Wittenberg in February and March of that year, that is, the rejection of infant baptism and a typical charismatic pneumatology.

We have a second example of women serving as ministers, this time from Mühlhausen, where preaching may again have been involved. After the defeat of the peasants' uprising a woman named Kreuter was publicly flogged to extract from her the whereabouts of her husband, but also because she was charged with celebrating Mass. A parenthetical remark reported that "she was instructed by Pfeifer."[33] This means that she was probably installed in office by Heinrich Pfeifer, a friend of Thomas Müntzer.

Any study of lay preachers would be incomplete without the better known names and cases for which we have accounts of what was written or said. So far mention has been made of Karsthans and Nikolaus Storch, of the latter in connection with the women preachers at Zwickau. We should add to those two the Peasant of Wöhrd and Sebastian Lotzer.

[32]Hoyer, "Zwickauer Storchianer," 69ff.
[33]*Akten zur Geschichte des Bauernkrieges*, 2: 753ff.

Reliable sources tell us that Nikolaus Storch preached in public and that he and most of his followers were clothmakers and journeymen in Zwickau. From the interrogation that took place in December 1521 and from reports on the Storchians visit to Wittenberg we are familiar with their spiritualist and eschatological notions.[34] We need to be critical of the idea that Storch propagated violence and insurrection, a sentiment we find in the *Vita Philippi Melanchtoni* published by Joachim Camerarius.[35] Storch remained active after the Peasants' War, and we find him in the center of a circle of laymen in Hof.[36] Information on the situation in Zwickau after 1522 suggests that some of his disciples continued to hold radical theological views. This did not, however, lead to renewed public preaching, nor is there a link with the local Anabaptist movement. With H. S. Bender in mind, but also with a slight polemic note, I have noted that the "Storchians" were a lay community during the early period of the Reformation under the influence not of Luther, but of Thomas Müntzer.[37] More research is needed in this connection into the roots of the *Secta Storchitarum* in the movement of the confraternities which was widespread in many Saxon towns, such as Zwickau, during the late Middle Ages.

Diepold Peringer, also known as the Peasant of Wöhrd, is cited as a typical example of a lay preacher in many narratives on the Reformation. There can be no doubt that he was extremely popular during the initial years of the Reformation, but if he was actually a layman is controversial. Clemen has provided evidence that Peringer was a monk who had deserted the monastery; if so, he was not necessarily ordained. According to Spalatin, the monastery in question was at Aichbaum.[38] We know of claims made by a woman that Peringer had once been her village priest.[39] That particular report came from E. Kreutzer, a goldsmith in Nürnberg and contemporary of Peringer, but beyond that there is no other confirmation. Under pressure from Archduke

---

[34]Especially Th. Kolde, "Ältester Bericht über die Zwickauer Propheten," *Zeitschrift für Kirchengeschichte* 5 (1882): 323ff and Ulrich Bubenheimer, "Luthers Stellung zum Aufruhr in Wittenberg 1520-1522 und die frühreformerischen Wurzeln des landesherrlichen Kirchenregiments," *Zeitschrift der Savigny-Stiftung für Rechtsgeschichte, Kan. Abt.* 101 (1985): 170ff.

[35]J. Camerarius, *De vita Philippi Melanchthonis. Rec. G. Th. Strobelius* (Halle, 1777). On Camerarius as propagator of the "Storch" legend see Max Steinmetz, *Das Müntzerbild von Luther bis Friedrich Engels* (Berlin, 1971), 64ff. On the roots of this charge regarding the use of force see also Hoyer, "Zwickauer Storchianer," 72.

[36]Paul Tschaekert, "Nicolaus Storch," *Allgemeine Deutsche Biographie*, vol. 36, (Leipzig, 1893), 442ff; Paul Wappler, *Die Täuferbewegung in Thüringen 1526-1584* (Jena, 1913), 186; Christian Meyer, "Der Wiedertäufer Nicolaus Storch und seine Anhänger in Hof, von Enoch Widmans handschriftlicher Chronik," *Zeitschrift für Kirchengeschichte* 16 (1896): 118ff.

[38]Clemen, "Der Bauer von Wöhrd," 86ff.

[39]G. E. Waldau, "Etwas von dem Bauern zu Wöhrd," *Vermischte Beyträge zur Geschichte der Stadt Nürnberg* 3 (1788), 23, 417.

Hoyer   95

Ferdinand the Nürnberg Council, after some hesitation, prohibited Peringer in February 1521 from further preaching. The reason probably was that many took him to be a preaching peasant, mostly on account of certain characteristic remarks he included in his speeches. There is good reason to assume that the council of the imperial city was frightened not only by Peringer's appeal but also by the fact that other lay preachers were appearing in the area.[40]

Otto Clemen has shown that Peringer's *Eyn sermon gepredigt vom Pawern zu Werdt*, first published by H. Höltzel in Nürnberg and reprinted several times, was closely related to the text of a pamphlet written by Benedictus Gretzinger, the town clerk of Reutlingen.[41] We also know of a complaint made by Peringer that not even half of his sermon had been printed.[42] This leaves ample room for speculation on what was left out and why. A later sermon preached by Peringer in Kitzingen, *Ein sermon von der Abgötterey. . .* was printed by Hans Hergot in Nürnberg in May of 1524. It is basically in agreement with Luther's views, and I find myself in agreement with Günter Vogler who first called attention to this fact. However, two reservations must be voiced—his blunt rejection of idolatry without calling for the destruction of images, and his general appreciation of the laity coupled with a disdain for academic education.[43]

This probably is why Luther speaks of Peringer as a follower of Karlstadt in a letter to Spalatin of April 10, 1525, long after Peringer had ceased preaching in the Nürnberg area. The reformer was also aware that Peringer was a monk pretending to be a peasant.[44]

Sebastian Lotzer, a journeyman furrier from Memmingen who was well versed in the Bible, is a borderline case as regards lay preaching.[45] He never preached in public but he interrupted Mass in the presence of conservative priests and held public disputations. On the question of lay preaching, he insisted that it was an aspect of priesthood. He expressly cited the model of Karsthans, the lay preacher, in his first writing entitled *Hailsame Ermanunge an*

---

[40]Günter Vogler, *Nürnberg: Studien zur Geschichte der reformatorischen und sozialen Bewegung in der Reichsstadt* (Berlin, 1982), 139. See also n33.

[41]Otto Clemen, "Bemerkungen zu Benedict Gretzingers Beschirmbüchlein," *Beiträge zur Reformationsgeschichte aus Büchern und Handschriften der Zwickauer Ratsschulbibliothek*, vol. 3 (Berlin, 1903), 25ff.

[42]Vogler, *Nürnberg*, 144.

[43]Especially "Es thut jn wol zörner/das jn eyn pawer die warheyt sagt, der nie auff keyner hohen schull gewesen ist/Denn so jns eyn doctor sagtt/So sprechen sie/Er ist auff eyner Hohenschull gestanden/Aber gott macht solch blind/töricht und unsinnig volck zu schanden." Cited in Vogler, *Nürnberg*, 146.

[44]WA Br 3:470. "et ut dicitur, Monachus simulato rustici vultu."

[45]Barbara B. Gerber, "Sebastian Lotzer, ein gelehrter Laie im Streit um das göttliche Recht," *Radikale Reformatoren: 21 biographische Skizzen von Thomas Müntzer bis Paracelsus*, ed. Hans-Jürgen Goertz (München, 1978), 60ff.

die ynwoner zu horw.[46] From the outset he combined criticism of the old church and its priests with social criticism. When he wrote that literate laymen should take the place of learned doctors he may have been within the framework of Luther's concept of the priesthood of all believers, but on the other hand, Lotzer did not mention the need for supervision or influence to be exercised by the congregation or the need for their confirmation of the preacher.

Lotzer expressly justified the tumultuous scenes which took place outside the Church of our Lady in Memmingen on December 25, 1524 in protest against the priests. He said that a community desired only what was holy and right. If the authorities acted similarly they could expect respect and obedience. But if there was a riot the responsibility lay with the priests who obstructed the spread of the gospel. Speaking of the events which had taken place in front of the Church of our Lady, he added that if these were seen as insurrection, then Christ had done the same.[47] One notes a clear divergence from Luther. Lotzer is closer to Zwingli who does not exclude the use of force when it comes to making the gospel a reality.

The involvement of the laity as preachers formed an integral part of the period we call the early Reformation. It arose from a broad and enthusiastic anti-Roman Catholic movement which spread through society; it was reinforced by the high esteem in which laymen were held by the humanists and particularly by Luther's concept of the priesthood of believers. Lay preaching clearly broke the monopoly of ordained priests and it helped mobilize large groups outside the priesthood to propagate the message of the reformers. It was fiercely resisted by the established church, by Catholic rulers and by town magistrates, which correctly saw it as subversive to the theological foundation of the traditional means of propagating the faith.

No accurate figures can be given on the number or proportion of lay preachers because of inadequate sources and often inaccurate statements about the previous occupations of the preachers. We do know that the preachers came from various social classes and included members of the clergy who were open to Reformation ideas, as well as monks who had been ordained. Unfortunately, we cannot draw inferences as to precise number and social positions of the lay preachers from the body of Lutheran ministers that was later established, since many lay preachers did not join the new evangelical church which emerged after the visitations.

Lay preachers who were either former monks or scholars of humanistic persuasion were generally close to Luther's theological positions. This facilitated their integration into regional Lutheran churches, in contrast to laymen and groups of laity who had been craftsmen or belonged to other urban social

---

[46]Adolf Laube, ed., *Flugschriften der frühen Reformationsbewegung (1518-1524)* (Berlin, 1983), 1:252.

[47]Sebastian Lotzer, *Schriften*, ed. A. Goetze (Leipzig, 1902), 82ff.

classes. Here a number of different social and theological factors were at work, including Karlstadt's high regard for manual labor and his disdain for academic education, and the preference given to the laity by Müntzer during his time in Zwickau. This is why there was a much larger number of lay preachers with an artisan background who took radical theological positions and combined theological and social demands. In so doing they expressed the social and religious concerns of the lower classes during the early Reformation.[48]

Radical lay preachers often enjoyed the support of a congregation, sometimes in opposition to the authorities, and of peasant alliances, which arose in the course of the peasants' uprising. Luther himself supported these radical aspirations in some of his writings as late as 1523, although Lutheran authorities had already begun to interfere with the activities of preaching laymen whose theological positions on significant issues diverged from Luther's Reformation, such as the Storchians in Zwickau and in other instances during the Peasants' War in Thuringia. This helps explain why Luther's writings after 1526 laid greater emphasis on ordination, which was put into practice by the emerging new church. Previous work has shown that many ministers of the regional evangelical churches were former craftsmen, but they (as all other preachers) were required to undergo elementary training which was nothing other than the teaching of Lutheran theology.[49]

Even though only few of the sermons preached by laymen have come down to us, their very existence and their radical note invite criticism of the findings of Bernd Moeller in his recent study of the content of sermons preached in German towns during the early Reformation.[50] Moeller concludes from text summaries that most sermons were in keeping with Luther's thought. This can, however, be demonstrated for only a fraction of the material. Our observations suggest that in some towns sermons were preached by both laymen and members of the regular and secular clergy which did not follow the Lutheran line. Their theological and social message was probably addressed mainly to the low and middle social classes, but under the keen surveillance of the urban authorities there was little chance of it being printed. Much detailed work certainly remains to be done here, but the uniformity of doctrine and "partisan spirit," to use Moeller's words again, would seem to have been limited in social terms to the property holding bourgeoisie.

---

[48]Robert Scribner, "Is There a Social History of Reformation?" *Social History* 2 (1977): 494ff.; Adolf Laube, "Die Reformation als soziale Bewegung," *Zeitschrift für Geschichtswissenschaft* 33 (1985): 428ff.

[49]Karant-Nunn, "Luther's Pastors," 11; Klaus, "Soziale Herkunft," 38ff.

[50]Moeller, "Was wurde in den deutschen Städten," 178ff, 192.

Diß ist die warhafftige gestalt vnd figur des Münsterischen Königs/des hand-
werds ein Schneyder/seines alters im. ʒʒvj. jar/ Mit person/farb/tleydung vnd wappen/wie hie steet/Welchen der
Bischoff gefangen vnd noch gefengklich enthelt/denselben auch also hat abconterfeen lassen/auch etlichen
Fürsten vnd Herren zü geschickt/Ist gemelter König seer truʒiger wort ꝛc. Es waiß auch noch
niemandt wie es jm ergeen oder was mit jm angefangen werden würdt.

Wer sich erhöcht in diser welt
Got achtet weder güt noch gelt

Auß dem stül würdt er gestossen
Bald müß er legen ein Blossen.

Hans Guldenmundt.

Jan van Leyden
From single-leaf woodcut by Erhard Schoen fl. Nuremburg, 1525–50)
98

The Anabaptist Kingdom of Münster in the Tension Between Anabaptism and Imperial Policy

Günter Vogler

IN THE FINAL CHAPTER OF HIS *GERMAN HISTORY in the Age of the Reformation*, after having characterized Paracelsus, Leopold von Ranke opined:

> At that time the general movement of minds was also linked with the attempt to shake off the yoke of strict discipline, the rule of the antique discipline, even church and state. Müntzer's inspirations, the socialist attempts of Anabaptism, and the theories of Paracelsus match very well. Had they been united, they would have reorganized the world. But they could not dominate after all; what prevented this was their internal confusion and profusion. They would have caused nothing but interrupting the great world-historic course of culture.[1]

These sentences need correction, but we cite them here because of Ranke's insistence that these ideas might have been capable of reorganizing the world. Although he immediately qualifies this possibility, he takes for granted that alternate thinking was articulated in them. Ranke does not explicitly mention the Anabaptist Kingdom in Münster in this connection, but his *German History* suggests the question of its place as an alternative to the prevailing social order.

The question is not new. But there was no possibility of a realistic and appropriate assessment of the Anabaptist rule in Münster as long as that reign was branded as heretical and was demonized, as long as the Anabaptist movement "one- sidedly had its radical wings clipped and was left out of consideration as to the still broader popular movement after the Peasants' War."[2]

After Marxist scholarship had stressed for a long time the inter-relationship between the Anabaptist movement and the continuation of traditions of the Peasants' War—as an attempt of its continuation or as a critical analysis of its legacy—the revision of more traditional views in Anabaptist

---

[1]Leopold von Ranke, *Deutsche Geschichte im Zeitalter der Reformation* (München, 1925), 5:293.

[2]Gerhard Zschäbitz, *Zur mitteldeutschen Wiedertäuferbewegung nach dem großen Bauernkrieg* (Berlin, 1958), 13.

research has created different points of departure. This, for example, is demonstrated by studies that prove personnel relations between the Anabaptist movement and the Peasants' War,[3] that analyze the Schleitheim Articles as a critical encounter with the experience of the Peasants' War,[4] that look into the role of the "common man" in the light of baptismal conceptions,[5] or that work out the varied relationships of Anabaptists towards violence.[6]

Meanwhile, a number of remarkable studies have contributed to "liberate the Anabaptist Kingdom in Münster from its scholarly-historical ghetto,"[7] making it possible to see this phenomenon again as an alternate option. Hans-Jürgen Goertz has described "The Alternatives of the Anabaptists" in the first chapter of his outline of a history of Anabaptism and what he has in mind is not only the differentiation of the Anabaptist movement but also how it embodied the search "for new forms of religious communication and social order"[8] which was based on the protest against ecclesiastical-social grievances.

The revision of the traditional image of the Anabaptists[9] shows—in view of the changed situation in scholarship—that the Anabaptist Kingdom at Münster is understood as an alternative, as expressed, for example, in Goertz's statement: "All in all, the Anabaptist theocracy saw itself as a 'counter-world' of the old Empire," thus as an alternate manifestation which "from outside" necessarily had "to be regarded as a provocation of the entire society."[10] Bernd Moeller, in turn, considers Münster as the example of "a radical and collective escape from the given world order" which had "a historical importance above and beyond the scope of local and temporary things due to its course and its shipwreck."[11]

---

[3]Gottfried Seebaß, "Bauernkrieg und Täufertum in Franken," *Zeitschrift für Kirchengeschichte* 85 (1974): 104ff; Claus-Peter Clasen, *Anabaptism: A Social History 1525-1618* (Ithaca: Cornell University Press, 1972), 152ff, 458ff.

[4]Hans-Jürgen Goertz, *Die Täufer: Geschichte und Deutung* (München, 1980), 20ff; Arnold Snyder, "The Schleitheim Articles in Light of the Revolution of the Common Man: Continuation or Departure?" *Sixteenth Century Journal* 16 (1985): 419ff.

[5]Werner O. Packull, "In Search of the 'Common Man' in Early German Anabaptist Theology," *Sixteenth Century Journal* 17 (1986): 51ff.

[6]James M. Stayer, *Anabaptists and the Sword* (Lawrence, KS: Coronado Press, 1972)

[7]Hans-Jürgen Goertz, "Zu dieser Nummer," *Mennonitische Geschichtsblätter* 40 n.r. 35 (1983): 6.

[8]Goertz, *Die Täufer*, 7.

[9]Ibid., 144ff.; Idem, "Das Täufertum—ein Weg in die Moderne?" in *Zwingli und Europa*, ed. Peter Blickle (Zürich, 1985), 167ff.; Abraham Friesen, "Social Revolution or Religious Reform? Some Salient Aspects of Anabaptist Historiography," in *Umstrittenes Täufertum 1525-1975*, ed. Hans-Jürgen Goertz (Göttingen, 1977), 223ff.; James M. Stayer, "Was Dr. Kuehler's Conception of Early Dutch Anabaptism Historically Sound? The Historical Discussion of Anabaptist Münster 450 Years Later," *Mennonite Quarterly Review* 60 (1986): 261-88.

[10]Goertz, *Die Täufer*, 35.

[11]Bernd Moeller, *Deutschland im Zeitalter der Reformation* (Göttingen, 1977), 102.

In light of such observations, the Anabaptist Kingdom regains its place in the history of the Anabaptist movement and belongs to the history of the Holy Roman Empire. From this point of view it is not a question of a local event, a peripheral matter, but a phenomenon that has its historical place at the beginning of the modern time.

That is why the following remarks focus on the place of the Anabaptist theocracy in the Anabaptist movement, and on its imperial-political relevance. Two questions will have priority: What expressed the radicalism of the Münster Anabaptists which was molded by apocalyptic ideas? What motives guided the estates of the Empire in their fight against the Anabaptist reign?

II

First, it is necessary to demarcate certain preconditions. Marxist historiography defines the period from the close of the fifteenth century onward as a time of transition from feudalism to capitalism.[12] On the one hand, we have feudal economic relations, social structures, political institutions, and social ideas. On the other hand, there developed within this society new elements in contradiction to such feudal foundations and expressed–in the long run–a bourgeois-capitalist system. The desire to overcome the existing social contradictions and to bring about the renewal of society received effective impetus through the Reformation and the Peasants' War in Germany. Certainly, the interests of the various class elements were differentiated and determined by differing motives, but they represented an alternative to church and society as those had been molded in the course of the formation and development of feudal society. Since the essential foundations of the feudal system were now jeopardized, opposed, and partly destroyed, it was the Reformation and the Peasants' War that showed their revolutionary explosive force. Consequently, it was a matter of class conflicts which present themselves as an early form of a bourgeois revolution.[13]

But, in light of the fact that the feudal powers defeated the peasants, after 1525 it was impossible to fight the rankling conflict in the way as had been the case during the Peasants' War. But the underlying causes of the conflict had not been eliminated, the social tensions continued to exist, and thus the reflection about a renewal of society increased. The changed conditions, which were largely determined by the defeat of the peasants in the Peasants' War, had to be taken into account, but, now as before, the reflection was rooted in the Reformation and the Peasants' War, as alternate ideas appear as confrontation with their consequences.

[12]Ranke, *Deutsche Geschichte*, vol. 3; Adolf Laube et al., *Die Epoche des Übergangs vom Feudalismus zum Kapitalismus von den siebziger Jahren des 15. Jahrhunderts bis 1789* (Berlin, 1983), 12ff.

[13]Adolf Laube et al., *Illustrierte Geschichte der deutschen frühbürgerlichen Revolution,* 2d ed. (Berlin, 1982).

What found expression in alternate ideas was, on the one hand, the disappointment with the course and the results of Luther's and Zwingli's Reformation. Hans Hut expressed this disappointment with the words that he had seen "that preaching at Wittenberg would not bring about a change for the better."[14] This was not an isolated opinion, but a voice in a polyphonic chorus.[15] This situation fostered and abetted the development and formation of the Anabaptist movement. On the other hand, alternate thinking was rooted in the recollection of the peasants' defeat which resulted in reflections as to how the goals not reached by them could be attained through other means. The unknown author of the pamphlet *About the New Change of a Christian Life* wrote

> I did not want to share with the peasants the profit they have realized due to their rebellion. I think it is justified that they received it. Do you not think that many scribes and other people of whom there are a great number in the world did wrong in the same way and the peasants did? And nobody shouts: stab, slay. But God, who is a true field bawler, is now moving along wanting to hit them, surely more drastically than the peasants. And they really carried on more drastically than the peasants. . . .[16]

The Peasants' War also left deep marks on Anabaptism.[17] What is striking is the extent to which apocalyptic notions, that were present in the late Middle Ages,[18] and also played a role in the early Reformation,[19] were voiced and now gained in importance. Werner O. Packull has described the conflicting nature of the attitudes related to apocalyptic expectations: "Paradoxically, the fervor of apocalyptic expectations appears to be symptomatic on the one hand

---

[14]Christian Meyer, "Zur Geschichte der Wiedertäufer in Oberschwaben," *Zeitschrift des Historischen Vereins für Schwaben und Neuburg* 1 (1874): 224

[15]Günter Vogler, *Nürnberg 1524/25: Studien zur Geschichte der reformatorischen und sozialen Bewegung in der Reichsstadt* (Berlin, 1982), 194ff.; Adolf Laube, "Ideal und Wirklichkeit. Zur Krisenstimmung in der Reformationsbewegung 1523/24," in *Martin Luther: Leben, Werk, Wirkung*, ed. Günter Vogler et al., 2d ed., (Berlin 1986), 91ff.

[16]Adolf Laube and Hans Werner Seiffert, eds., *Flugschriften der Bauernkriegszeit* (Berlin, 1975), 556.

[17]James M. Stayer, "Neue Modelle eines gemeinsamen Lebens," in *Alles gehört allen. Das Experiment Gütergemeinschaft vom 16. Jahrhundert bis heute*, ed. Hans-Jürgen Goertz (München, 1984), 29.

[18]Walter Schmithals, *Die Apokalyptik. Einführung und Deutung* (Göttingen, 1973); Bernhard McGinn, *Visions of the End: Apocalyptic Traditions in the Middle Ages* (New York: Columbia University Press, 1979).

[19]Ulrich Asendorf, *Eschatologie bei Luther* (Göttingen, 1967); Ole Modalsli, "Luther und die letzten Dinge," in *Leben und Werk Martin Luthers von 1526 bis 1546*, ed. Helmar Junghans, (Berlin, 1983), 1: 331ff.

of a hopeless situation, on the other hand of continued hope for change in the entire social structure."[20]

The desire for the "reformation of life"[21] (*Besserung des Lebens*) integrated various conceptions of a radically changed world. The promise of a new heaven and a new earth (Isa. 65:17) and of a New Jerusalem (Rev. 21:2) offered models. Thus apocalyptic, eschatological, and chiliastic expectations were the potential for alternate thinking. This was not only typical of Anabaptism as a whole, but also of an influential current represented by Hans Hut, Augustin Bader, and Melchior Hoffman that led to Dutch Melchioritism and the Anabaptism of Münster. What cannot be overlooked in this connection is that "the stronger the chiliastic-eschatological momentum, the more dangerous for society became Anabaptism and the faster there occurred change to rebellious religious militancy rather than the quietist negation of the world and sectarian isolation."[22]

Balthasar Hubmaier implored in 1527, "Oh my Lord Jesus Christ, shorten the days and come down soon."[23] The expectation of the Second Coming is present here without pinpointing the date and the hour of the event. It seems that God revealed his plan to others because they dated the apocalyptic event and forecasted its course. Hans Hut, eyewitness of the Peasants' War and follower of Thomas Müntzer, effectively articulated the apocalyptic expectation.[24] Gerhard Zschäbitz refers to this with this reflection:

Hut's great missionary successes seem to be due to the fact that in a time of revolutionary excitement chiliastic ideas with impending "dates" of change played a greater role in the thinking of the "common people" than the resigning, passive, inner-worldly asceticism demanded by other Anabaptist apostles.[25]

[20]Packull, "In Search of the 'Common Man,'" 66.

[21]Goertz, *Die Täufer*, 67ff.

[22]Gerhard Brendler, *Das Täuferreich zu Münster 1534/35* (Berlin, 1966), 102.; for a similar argument see also Zschäbitz, *Zur mitteldeutschen Wiedertäuferbewegung*, 63.

[23]Balthasar Hubmaier, *Schriften*, ed. Gunnar Westin and Torsten Bergsten (Gütersloh, 1962), 218.

[24]Gottfried Seebaß, "Müntzers Erbe, Werk, Leben und Theologie des Hans Hut," (Theol. Habil., Erlangen, 1972); Idem, "Das Zeichen der Erwählten. Zum Verständnis der Taufe bei Hans Hut," in *Umstrittenes Täufertum*, 138ff; Zschäbitz, *Zur mitteldeutschen Wiedertäuferbewegung*, 49ff; Hans-Dieter Schmid, "Das Hutsche Täufertum. Ein Beitrag zur Charakterisierung einer täuferischen Richtung aus der Frühzeit der Täuferbewegung," *Historisches Jahrbuch* 91 (1971): 327ff.; Stayer, *Anabaptists and the Sword*, 150ff.; Werner O. Packull, *Mysticism and the Early South German-Austrian Anabaptist Movement 1525-1531* (Scottdale: Herald Press, 1977), 62ff.

[25]Zschäbitz, *Zur mitteldeutschen Wiedertäuferbewegung*, 63.

Augustin Bader saw himself as a prophet sent by God.[26] According to his examination records he taught his followers that he had been sent by God to be a king and that he had been ordered through visions and signs "to announce a change of the world everywhere and to win domination over the entire world verywhere."[27] There is a direct line from Hut and Bader to Melchior Hoffman[28] who considered it impossible to build the New Jerusalem unless Babylon had been overthrown.[29]

In comparison with the concretely articulated social, legal, and political demands of the time of the Peasants' War, the pursuit of a comprehensive change dissolved into vague expectations and the demand for the relief of the "common people" from the burdens of feudal exploitation evaporated into a hope for a better world. This expressed a loss of a sense of reality. On the other hand, resorting to apocalyptic visions is evidence of a blatant increase in radicalism which found its expressions in the expectations of the Kingdom of Heaven. Although from time to time small groups tried to take into account the apocalyptic expectations through their actions,[30] the Anabaptist claim to be different (*Anderssein*) manifested itself largely in the formation of congregations as alternate forms of living.[31]

The rejection of the "world," which remained an Anabaptist characteristic, meant an insult to clerical and secular authorities.[32] The attempt at "separation" from society had to be viewed as a challenge to feudal or urban society. The persecutions were the response of authorities who felt threatened.[33]

The Anabaptist expectations were realized in clandestine congregations which reflected the life of small communities according to their own chosen standards of following Christ. Exceptions were—on the one hand—the Hutterites in Moravia tolerated by the authorities[34] and—on the other

---

[26]Ibid., 65ff.; Packull, *Mysticism*, 130ff.; Richard van Dülmen, *Reformation als Revolution: Soziale Bewegung und religiöser Radikalismus in der deutschen Reformation* (München, 1977), 226ff.

[27]Paul Wappler, *Die Täuferbewegung in Thüringen von 1526 bis 1584* (Jena, 1913), 316ff.

[28]Klaus Deppermann, *Melchior Hoffman: Soziale Unruhen und apokalyptische Visionen im Zeitalter der Reformation* (Göttingen, 1979); Idem, "Melchior Hoffmans Weg von Luther zu den Täufern," in *Umstrittenes Täufertum*, 173ff.; Brendler, *Das Täuferreich zu Münster*, 105ff.; Stayer, *Anabaptists and the Sword*, 211ff.; Cornelius Krahn, *Dutch Anabaptism* (The Hague, 1968), 80ff.

[29]Manfred Krebs and Hans-Georg Rott, eds., *Quellen zur Geschichte der Wiedertäufer, Elsaß 2. Stadt Straßburg 1533-1535.* (Gütersloh, 1960), 393.

[30]Zschäbitz, *Zur mitteldeutschen Wiedertäuferbewegung*, 65ff.

[31]Clasen, *Anabaptism*, 62ff.; Goertz, *Die Täufer*, 98ff.; James M. Stayer, "Die Anfänge des schweizerischen Täufertums im reformierten Kongregationalismus," in *Umstrittenes Täufertum*, 19ff.; Martin Haas, "Der Weg der Täufer in die Absonderung. Zur Interdependenz von Theologie und sozialem Verhalten," in *Umstrittenes Täufertum*, 50ff.

[32]Hans Joachim Hillerbrand, *Die politische Ethik des oberdeutschen Täufertums: Eine Untersuchung zur Religions- und Geistesgeschichte des Reformationszeitalters* (Leiden/Köln, 1962).

[33]Clasen, *Anabaptism*, 358ff; Goertz, *Die Täufer*, 127ff.

[34]Clasen, *Anabaptism*, 210ff.

hand—the Anabaptists at Münster who took over control of a large town, abolished the old forms of governance, and molded society according to the Scriptural model.

III

In Münster we face the phenomenon that apocalyptic expectations and their realization coincide with the active behavior of the people. The event in a way mirrors the "radicalization of the radicals" which is expressed in several perspectives:

a) Passing through Luther's and Zwingli's Reformations and their repudiation, this radicalization becomes apparent in the notion that restitution began with Luther but needed to be completed.

b) It is reflected in the formation of the specific theology represented by Bernhard Rothmann as the ideological basis of the Anabaptist Kingdom.

c) It is documented in the destruction of the old order, the establishment of the Anabaptist reign, and its organization as New Jerusalem.

The conditions that made this development possible have been repeatedly described in the literature:[35] the local traditions of the town's struggle for autonomy, the economic crisis manifested in economic ties to the Netherlands; the town's burdens arising from the repeated episcopal successions; the chronic conflict between the bishop and the town as well as between the City Council and the people; the influence of the Reformation and its autonomous acceptance; the formation of an Anabaptist congregation, and its link with the municipal Reformation.[36]

Thus a whole set of factors expressed specific conditions under which it was possible for Anabaptism to gain a foothold in Münster and "here a religious group really awaited Christ's return, the Day of Judgement, and the imminent end of the world—according to scriptural prophecies."[37]

The theological foundation was laid by the preacher Bernhard Rothmann who moved beyond the ideas of Melchior Hoffman and the Dutch Melchiorites.[38] Although previous writings evoked eschatological

---

[35]Heinz Schilling, "Aufstandsbewegungen in der stadtbürgerlichen Gesellschaft des Alten Reiches. Die Vorgeschichte des Münsteraner Täuferreiches, 1525 bis 1534," in *Der deutsche Bauernkrieg 1524-1526*, ed. Hans-Ulrich Wehler (Göttingen, 1975), 193ff.; Otthein Rammstedt, *Sekte und soziale Bewegung: Soziologische Analyse der Täufer in Münster 1534/35* (Köln/Opladen, 1966), 15ff.; van Dülmen, *Reformation als Revolution*, 258ff.

[36]James M. Stayer, "Theses on the Position of the Münster Kingdom in the History of Anabaptism" (MS); Heinz Schilling, "Aufstandsbewegungen," 208ff.

[37]Karl-Heinz Kirchhoff, "Die Endzeiterwartung der Täufergemeinde zu Münster 1534/35: Gemeindebildung unter dem Eindruck biblischer Verheißungen," *Jahrbuch für Westfälische Kirchengeschichte* 78 (1985): 19.

[38]Martin Brecht, "Die Theologie Bernhard Rothmanns," Jahrbuch für Westfälische Kirchengeschichte 78 (1985): 49ff.; Deppermann, *Melchior Hoffman*, 296ff.

expectations,[39] he unfolded his apocalyptic view comprehensively in his writings of 1534 and 1535. This is true of the *Restitution of the True and Sound Christian Doctrine* of October 1534, the *Report on Wrath* of December 1534, *On the Secrecy of the Writing of the Kingdom of Christ* of February 1535, and the tract *On Worldly and Spiritual Power* which is preserved incompletely. Rothmann himself mentioned the apocalyptic roots by writing, "where the restitution shall happen—for this read all the prophets and particularly the Apocalypse as well as the fourth book of Ezra." And he added that those who want to know should read Isaiah, Jeremiah, Ezekiel, and Daniel, the twelve Minor Prophets, Ezra 4, the Psalms, the Apocalypse, and Christ's parables.[40]

Rothmann interpreted history—which he, of course, considered to be the history of salvation—as a succession of apostasy and restitution.[41] The apostasy from God happened because "the people thought exceedingly of their own wisdom and pleasures instead of showing steadfastness in following Christ's teaching."[42] In another connection he developed his conception of the three worlds. The first world disappeared in water, namely through the Flood; the second, the present world, will perish by fire and be purified by it; the third world will be the New Heaven and the New Earth in which the people will live in justice.[43]

Rothmann saw the Kingdom of Christ as the goal of history. He held it to be certain and conclusive that Christ will return in his glory at the end of the second world in order to hold court and to treat everybody according to his merits.[44]

> For, after the burning down of heaven and earth and the bursting of the elements, the New Heaven and the New Earth shall appear before the people of God and justice shall live there. Thereupon shall be peace on the whole world, all creatures shall be free for the glory of God's children.[45]

Rothmann considered this to be the third world, the perfect one.[46]

---

[39]Robert Stupperich, ed., *Die Schriften Bernhard Rothmanns* (Münster, 1970), 24; Brecht, "Die Theologie Bernhard Rothmanns," p. 69ff.

[40]Stupperich, *Die Schriften Bernhard Rothmanns*, 355; see also p. 368.

[41]John H. Yoder, "Anabaptism and History: 'Restitution' and the Possibility of Renewal," in *Umstrittenes Täufertum*, 244ff.

[42]Stupperich, *Die Schriften Bernhard Rothmanns*, 216.

[43]Ibid., 346.

[44]Ibid., 350.

[45]Ibid., 296; see also 352, 364.

[46]Ibid., 337.

Restitution is the reparation of apostasy. It is the time of the establishment of all those things which God has ever mentioned through the voices of his prophets. Restitution is the beginning of the time of vengeance that now has come. Rothmann refuted arguments that God will come down from heaven, with his angels, in order to destroy the godless. It is true that God will come "but vengeance is a prior task of the servants of God. . . . We have to be his tools and must attack the godless on the days that the Lord will determine."[47]

Rothmann held that the time of salvation and restitution began with the Reformation when God awakened Luther, but it had not yet been concluded. Thus there is a line from the learned men Erasmus, Luther, and Zwingli to the non-learned ones, i.e. Melchior Hoffman, Jan Matthijs, and Jan van Leiden.[48] In this time of restitution God will rally his people in order to put an end to godless manners. The earth will be occupied and be at the command of Christ, the King of the whole world. The "wrong order" shall be eliminated, for, although governmental authority was a God-ordained order, "this order has long been wrong because the authorities not only forgot their duties and took unfair advantages but also turned against God himself and his word."[49]

A consequence of Rothmann's theology was the radical reorganization of society (it is unimportant, in this connection, if Rothmann thought ahead to what might happen or if he subsequently legitimized what had happened). If the authorities had "inverted" the God-given order, this inversion in fact meant its reorganization. In Münster this happened step by step, but at a speedy pace.[50] The internal situation and the isolation because of the siege also motivated action on the following matters of principle:

> Making Christ's congregation perfect, fulfilling the Father's will which he has declared through the prophets, i.e. to live in a way completely different from that of the feudal world around them and to emulate the patriarchs of the Old Testament—this is what made the leaders of the Anabaptist Kingdom look for ever new ways and means of adapting the internal conditions of Münster to the scriptural model.[51]

This model was the promised New Jerusalem which was mentioned for the first time by a joiner's wife on February 8, 1534, during the calls for

[47]Ibid., 292.

[48]Ibid., 219.

[49]Ibid., 277.

[50]Eike Wolgast, "Herrschaftsorganisation und Herrschaftskrisen im Täuferreich von Münster 1534/35," *Archiv für Reformationsgeschichte* 67 (1976): 179ff.; van Dülmen, *Reformation als Revolution*, 285ff.

[51]Brendler, *Das Täuferreich zu Münster*, 132.

penance.[52] Anabaptists won the City Council elections on February 23, thus lawfully assuming power, which enabled them to pursue Anabaptist policies. The Council remained the instrument of executive power, but it stood in the shadow of the prophetic actions of Jan Matthijs.[53] It was during this phase that the idea of the purity of the community of the saints brought about the expulsion of those of different beliefs and the first steps towards the reform of ownership relations.[54]

Matthijs died on April 5, 1534, and the constitution of the Council which had epitomized the old urban rule was abolished. Jan van Leiden established a "Council of the Twelve Elders of the Tribes of Israel." Hermann Kerssenbroick reported on this event, "He called these twelve men the elders of the tribes of Israel in whom should be vested jurisdiction over all public and private, spiritual, and secular matters, as well as power over life and death and the supreme governmental power."[55] Thus, the old constitution was abolished and a move towards a scriptural model had been made.[56] Rules for the common life were issued. The first article read, "What the Bible commands or prohibits shall be observed under penalty by all Israelites."[57] Also, polygamous matrimony was introduced during this phase.

After the repulsion of the second attack on the town on August 31, 1534 this constitution of the elders was abolished and replaced by the kingdom of Jan van Leiden.[58] The prophesies of the establishment of the New Jerusalem were now considered to have come true and—as a sign—the cathedral yard was renamed "Mount Zion." The rules for the town issued on January 2, 1535 were better aligned to military requirements, in view of the ongoing siege.

The claim to represent the New Jerusalem was expressed outwardly by Jan van Leiden's assumption of the title of king, with royal insignia, and royal retinue. The new reign was based on the principle of obedience to the new rule. Hermann Kerssenbroick reported "And reading the thirteenth chapter of the Epistle to the Romans they determinedly urged everyone to obey."[59] Of course, the New Jerusalem needed an internal order, particularly in light of the siege. The reference to Romans 13 did not violate the principle of viewing the gospel as guideline. But one cannot fail to notice that they had to give the same legitimation to the exhortation to obedience as the feudal rule had done

---

[52]Kirchhoff, "Die Endzeiterwartung," 30.

[53]Wolgast, "Herrschaftsorganisation," 181.

[54]Brendler, *Das Täuferreich zu Münster*, 115ff.; Kirchhoff, "Die Endzeiterwartung," 25ff.

[55]Richard van Dülmen, ed., *Das Täuferreich zu Münster 1534/35. Berichte und Dokumente* (München, 1974), 113.

[56]Brendler, *Das Täuferreich zu Münster*, 128ff.; Wolgast, "Herrschaftsorganisation," 182ff.

[57]van Dülmen, *Das Täuferreich zu Münster 1534/35*, 116.

[58]Brendler, *Das Täuferreich zu Münster*, 143ff.; Wolgast, "Herrschaftsorganisation," 186ff.

[59]van Dülmen, *Das Täuferreich zu Münster 1534/35*, 149.

earlier. The constitution of the Council and of the elders was related to the town of Münster, and even if Jan van Leiden considered himself to be the "king over the whole world," his real sphere of rule was the town. He had twelve dukes elected in May 1535 to whom were assigned several territories of the Empire. This measure was obviously aimed at preparing the rule over these territories after an Anabaptist victory.[60] This political-geographical area bordered on the Elbe river and the Erz Mountains to the Northeast and the Main river to the South. This essentially included the North German and Dutch regions.[61] "The utopia of world domination was limited to the control of a part of the Holy Roman Empire beyond which the King's horizon of expectations did not reach."[62]

The universal claim announced in Jan van Leiden's coat of arms–a globe pierced by two swords and crowned by the cross[63]–remained beyond reality, even though it expressed consistent reflection in terms of the scriptural motivation. The Anabaptist reign could only be implemented within the city walls of Münster. But it was here that–under the banner of the restitution–the old order was rejected and replaced by a new constitution determined by the will of God, "an outright mirror image of the political and social world surrounding it."[64] The Anabaptist exercise of power, the partial dissolution of traditional ownership relations and the destruction of title-deeds, the adoption of new constitutions, the creation of specific institutions with their own legislation and jurisdiction signaled the destruction of feudal and, for that matter, urban power relationships. The old symbols of power were eradicated through iconoclasm or were systematically changed.[65]

Jan van Leiden as king had sword, sceptre, and orb carried before him, a striking expression of the royal dignity he claimed. These and other attributes, on the one hand, showed Münster to be a theocracy, and, on the other, characterized it as a secular order with its own insignia, coats of arms, seals, and currency. It is likely that the coins were aimed primarily at propagandistic purposes since they were not circulated in the town. The newly minted coins were intended to be valid in the whole world[66] and they did not only disseminate Jan van Leiden's effigy but also the message of the Anabaptists at Münster:

---

[60]Brendler, *Das Täuferreich zu Münster*, 157ff.

[61]Ibid., 158.

[62]Wolgast, "Herrschaftsorganisation," 200.

[63]Günter Vogler, "Das Täuferreich zu Münster im Spiegel der Flugschriften," in *Flugschriften als Massenmedium der Reformationszeit*, ed. Hans-Joachim Köhler (Stuttgart, 1981), 343 (Abb. Nr. 11), 344 (Abb. Nr. 12), 347 (Abb.Nr. 13), 348 (Abb. Nr. 14).

[64]Goertz, "Das Täufertum–ein Weg in die Moderne?" p. 175.

[65]Martin Warnke, "Durchbrochene Geschichte? Die Bilderstürme der Wiedertäufer in Münster 1534/35," in *Bildersturm. Die Zerstörung des Kunstwerks*, ed. Martin Warnke (München 1973), 75ff.

[66]van Dülmen, *Das Täuferreich zu Münster 1534/35*, 123.

"The Word was made flesh and lives among us. He who is not born of water and the Holy Spirit cannot enter the Kingdom of God. For there is only one true king over everyone, one God, one faith, one baptism."[67]

It may be astonishing that so many familiar elements from feudal society can be found in the New Jerusalem. But the God-given new order had to take a shape that related to human imaginative faculties. At the same time, it had to use traditional symbols if it wanted to appear legitimate in the eyes of its opponents. Thus, on the one hand, apocalyptic events found expression in institutional forms and, on the other hand, "an order oriented by the princely environment of the sixteenth century" was created.[68] Robert Stupperich considered this "phony apocalyptic reality" to be a "cruel deception."[69] But if we take the intentions of the Anabaptists of Münster seriously we must accept the notion that the apocalyptic events had to be understandable to them, and this is what they practiced step by step.

The New Jerusalem was a new social order that existed and was based on scriptural principles which radically broke with the feudal world. What we observe is not the realization of a chiliastic idea but "an inner-worldly chiliastic or– strictly speaking–even pre-chiliastic realization before the Day of Judgment."[70] In this connection we must accept Karl-Heinz Kirchhoff's assessment that the measures "were to make it possible for a group of the elect to survive in a hostile environment until the time when the returning Christ would take over power in his kingdom of peace."[71]

IV

The radicalization of theology, the destruction of the old order, and a rule without feudal legitimation meant a challenge of clerical and secular forces, of Catholic and Protestant theologians as well as municipal and territorial authorities. Although Catholic and evangelical theologians intensively indulged in polemics against the Anabaptist tenets of the Münster representatives,[72] and the Bishop of Münster, supported by several rulers of neighboring territories, organized the siege of the town, it took sixteen months before the Anabaptist rule was overthrown. It is necessary to deal with

---

[67]Brendler, *Das Täuferreich zu Münster*, 147.

[68]Wolgast, "Herrschaftsorganisation," 188.

[69]Robert Stupperich, "Die Münstersche Apokalypse 1535," *Jahrbuch des Vereins für Westfälische Kirchengeschichte*, 53/54 (1960/61): 41.

[70]Brecht, "Die Theologie Bernhard Rothmanns," 78; see also Ferdinand Seibt, *Utopia, Modelle totaler Sozialplanung* (Düsseldorf, 1972), 191ff.

[71]Kirchhoff, "Die Endzeiterwartung," 20.

[72]Robert Stupperich, ed., *Schriften von katholischer Seite gegen die Täufer* (Münster, 1980); Idem, *Schriften von evangelischer Seite gegen die Täufer* (Münster, 1983); Günter Vogler, "Martin Luther und das Täuferreich zu Münster," in *Martin Luther: Leben, Werk, Wirkung*, 235ff.

the political constellation in the Empire in order to understand why it was possible for the Anabaptist rule to hold out for such a long time.

When the Anabaptists established their reign in Münster, the focus of the Habsburg dynasty and the German estates of the Empire was on other trouble spots.[73] This was particularly true of the Southwest where a new situation developed through the restoration of Ulrich of Württemberg to his duchy. In 1519, after a raid on the town of Reutlingen, the Swabian League had expelled the Duke from his land. It had come under Austrian rule which had made it possible for the Habsburg dynasty to establish an outpost to exert greater influence in Germany. Landgrave Philipp of Hesse worked for Duke Ulrich's return to his territory and undertook the necessary diplomatic and military steps to prepare for such action. As a result of the defeat of King Ferdinand's troops in the Battle of Lauffen on May 13, 1534, the ground was prepared for the return. On June 29 a treaty was signed in Kaaden (Kadán) near Eger in Northern Bohemia. As a result, Luther's sphere of influence was extended, the South German Reformation was restrained, and the "princely Reformation" strengthened.

At approximately the same time the political and reform conflicts in North Germany reached their culmination in the key Hanseatic town of Lübeck.[74] There the Bourgeois opposition secured the acceptance of several reform demands, the participation in municipal administration, and—finally in 1533—the election of the non-patrician merchant Jürgen Wullenwever as mayor. Lübeck which had been ousted from its position as mediator in the Baltic Sea trade now sought to reestablish its predominance. But the "counts' feud" (*Grafenfehde*), Lübeck's war against Denmark which began in May 1534, resulted in defeat. The Peace of Hamburg of February 14, 1536 recognized the Hanseatic privileges, but Lübeck did not regain its dominance in the Baltic region. At the same time a restructuring of the political alliances took place in the Empire, influenced by the Württemberg issue and, even more so, by the Reformation in general. In 1525 the Swabian League had worked for the suppression of the peasants' movements in South Germany but after the Peasants' War the diverging interests of the members of the League became more clearly apparent, provoked by the different attitudes of its members. The dissolution of the League was a particular goal of Philipp of Hesse. Despite Habsburg efforts the Swabian League that expired on February 2, 1534 was not renewed. The League failed in view of the disagreements over Württemberg (Habsburg as well as Hesse were members), the rivalry between

---

[73]Günter Vogler, "Die Jahre 1534/35–Kulminationsphase oder Krisenzeit der reformatorischen Bewegung im Reich und in Westeuropa?" in *Etat et religion aux XVe et XVIe siècles*, ed. W. P. Blockmans und Herman van Nufel (Brussels, 1986), 209ff.

[74]Günter Korell, *Jürgen Wullenwever: Sein sozial-politisches Wirken in Lübeck und der Kampf mit den erstarkenden Mächten Nordeuropas* (Weimar, 1980).

the Habsburg and Wittelsbach dynasties (Bavaria was among those which rejected Ferdinand's election as Roman king), and the prolonged resistance of several territories against the recognition of Ferdinand's election as Roman king.[75] Only in the Kaaden Treaty did the Elector of Saxony declare his readiness to recognize Ferdinand provisionally, even as Duke Ulrich indicated his acceptance of the Roman king. On the basis of the Treaty of Linz, of September 11, 1534, Bavaria pursued a policy of reconciliation with the Habsburg dynasty.

At the same time religious and confessional interests came more clearly to the fore in the context of efforts towards political alliances. This trend culminated in the formation of the Schmalkaldic League as a Protestant defensive alliance, with virtually all signatories of the Confessio Augustana reaching agreement on February 27, 1531. The sphere of influence of the Schmalkaldic League was broadened by new members in the mid-thirties, and for a while the League could count on support by France and England. But neither alliance included Northwest Germany and thus it was impossible to act against Münster.

What must also be considered is that in this phase the advocates of the Reformation in several towns pushed the respective councils to a decision concerning ecclesiastical change. This became evident in the course of the Reformation in North Germany [76] as well as in the South where such important towns as the imperial cities of Frankfurt and Augsburg took the decisive step of accepting the Reformation.[77] Both cities explained the Council decision in favor of the Reformation by saying that unrest and uproar of the "common man" would otherwise occur. As a result the authorities' influence on the structure of the Reformation increased.

Thus, the areas of conflict in the Southwest and in the North of the Empire were of primary interest. The third area of conflict—Münster and Northwest of the Empire—was, so to speak, peripheral. The Württemberg issue engaged the forces of the Habsburg dynasty and several rulers, the

---

[75]Alfred Kohler, *Antihabsburgische Politik in der Epoche Karls V. Die reichsständische Opposition gegen die Wahl Ferdinands I. zum römischen König und gegen die Anerkennung seines Königtums, 1524-1534* (Göttingen, 1982).

[76]Johannes Schildhauer, *Soziale, politische und religiöse Auseinandersetzungen in den Hansestädten Stralsund, Rostock und Wismar im ersten Drittel des 16. Jahrhunderts* (Weimar, 1959), 117ff.

[77]Sigrid Jahns, *Frankfurt, Reformation und Schmalkaldischer Bund: Die Täufer-, Reichs- und Bündnispolitik der Reichsstadt Frankfurt am Main 1525-1536* (Frankfurt/Main, 1976), 202ff.; Philip Broadhead, "Politics and Expediency in the Augsburg Reformation," in *Reformation Principle and Practice: Essays in Honour of Arthur Geoffrey Dickens*, ed. Peter N. Brooks (London, 1980), 55ff.; idem, "Popular Pressure for Reform in Augsburg, 1524-1534," in *Stadtbürgertum und Adel in der Reformation. Studien zur Sozialgeschichte der Reformation in England und Deutschland*, ed. Wolfgang J. Mommsen et al. (Stuttgart, 1979), 80ff.

Hanseatic towns were fixed on their confrontation with Denmark, the Swabian League was in the South and about to disintegrate, the Schmalkaldic League stressed its defensive character, and it was difficult to bring to bear the authority of the Emperor on these issues in view of the fact that he was absent. Since the interests of Burgundy, Cleves, and Hesse interfered with each other in the Northwest,[78] it appeared that the region was more or less paralyzed by rivaling forces and free space was created for the Anabaptist rule. Although the Bishop of Münster took pains to win the support of the rulers of neighboring territories, this was insufficient to fight against the Anabaptist rule effectively and capture the town. To accomplish this, the support of the estates of the Empire was necessary. This reality caused the Anabaptist Kingdom to become an element of imperial policy.

So far no scholarly study has examined what the public in the Empire knew about events in Münster and, above all, how the Anabaptists in towns and regions responded. There was an opportunity to obtain information by means of "newspapers"—actually pamphlets circulated in printed form.[79] They were placed on the market from the fall of 1534 until shortly after the capture of Münster. They disseminated all kinds of news about what was happening in and around the besieged town. Of course, the "newspapers" were aimed predominantly at warning against the "horrible happening," but the readers could also inform themselves how the Anabaptist successfully and cleverly defended their theocracy.

The rulers in the Empire also watched events intensively. They considered the apocalyptically motivated actions a real danger for the feudal order in the immediate vicinity and environs of Münster.[80] They continuously corresponded with each other, negotiated, and made arrangements in order to avert danger. This is documented by many gatherings—from the diet at Orsoy on March 26, 1534 when envoys of the Duke of Cleves and of the Elector of Cologne met with those of the Bishop of Münster, to other princely and electoral diets, assemblies of the Northern Rhenish Westphalian region and the Rhenish League to the diet of the three Rhenish circles in Coblenz on December 13-26, 1534 and the diet of the estates of the Empire at Worms of April 4-27, 1535.[81] Since it was impossible for the Bishop of Münster to continue

[78]Franz Petri, "Nordwestdeutschland im Wechselspiel der Politik Karls V. und Philipps des Großmütigen von Hessen," *Zeitschrift des Vereins für hessische Geschichte und Landeskunde* 71 (1960): 44ff.

[79]Vogler, "Das Täuferreich zu Münster im Spiegel der Flugschriften," p. 309ff.

[80]Günter Vogler, "Das Täuferreich zu Münster als Problem der Politik im Reich. Beobachtungen anhand reichsständischer Korrespondenzen der Jahre 1534/35," *Mennonitische Geschichtsblätter*, 42 (1985): 10ff.

[81]Karl-Heinz Kirchhoff, "Die Belagerung und Eroberung Münsters 1534/35. Militärische Maßnahmen und politische Verhandlungen des Fürstbischofs Franz von Waldeck," *Westfälische Zeitschrift* 112 (1962): 94ff.; Helmut Neuhaus, "Das Reich und die Wiedertäufer von Münster," *Westfälische Zeitschrift* 133 (1983): 16ff.

the siege without assistance and as the support given by rulers of the neighboring territories was inadequate, eventually most of the estates were mobilized to provide financial aid.

It is obvious that the rulers were interested in regaining Münster and reestablishing the old order. The bishop and the knights of the chapter did not tire of repeating the messages of the rulers that the Anabaptists had not only brought the town under their sway but also had "definitely destroyed all divine Christian order, jurisdiction, law, spiritual, and secular rule and police."[82] And, of course, it was considered abominable that Jan van Leiden had usurped the office of king. Thus the estates assembled at Coblenz reproached the Münsterites in a letter with "having raised a man from the tailor's trade to be an alleged king and having established many unchristian and unseemly statutes to spread the same over all regions of the Roman Empire and the entire Christian world."[83]

The Anabaptists of Münster, in turn, took steps to disseminate their teachings beyond the walls of the town, in line with the universal character of the apocalyptic events: "The Anabaptists of Münster believed that God had miraculously revealed that they were given the sword for an apocalyptic crusade through which the world would be punished and their kingdom made universal."[84] It is true enough that it was out of the question to translate intention into reality, but the authorities deeply feared an extension of the movement to other territories of the Empire.

As early as January 20, 1535 the Bishop of Münster wrote Landgrave Philipp of Hesse that this uprising would "make some progress with the common man and in other towns of our and neighboring countries."[85] The Anabaptists in the Empire were widely said to have revolutionary intentions so that persecution by the secular authorities could be justified. The same line of argumentation was used in the case of Münster, for example in the instruction for the district assembly at Cologne in October 1534. It was the Anabaptists' intention "to incite general insurrection and uprising in the Holy Empire, . . . to eradicate and suppress completely all authority and honesty, Christian religion, concord, and peace."[86]

This was the line of argument pursued in all further considerations to assist the Bishop. On April 26, 1535 the estates of the Empire assembled at Worms wrote King Ferdinand that if Münster was not taken with support from the whole Empire the Anabaptists and their followers would be

[82]Carl Adolf Cornelius, ed., *Berichte der Augenzeugen über das Münsterische Wiedertäuferreich* (Münster, 1853), 283.

[83]Stupperich, *Die Schriften Bernhard Rothmanns*, 413.

[84]Stayer, *Anabaptists and the Sword*, 239

[85]Cornelius, *Berichte der Augenzeugen*, 218.

[86]Ibid., 284.

strengthened in their unchristian, despotic attitude and . . . all the more induced . . . to suppress and wipe out all authority and honesty. From this will result irreversible disadvantage and damage, secession, uprising, and insurrection of the common man towards Imperial and Royal Majesty, the Holy Roman Empire, and all of its estates, and will finally lead to the ruin and disruption of the Roman Empire and of all authority and honesty.[87]

Thus, in 1534/35 the attention of the estates was eminently focused on the possible dangers emanating from Münster. A revolt of the "common man" was again and again conjured up and the Peasants' War was recalled, particularly since events in the Netherlands gave rise to such fears.[88] In this respect the Anabaptist Kingdom was not only opposed in order to reestablish the old clerical and political order in Münster but also to prevent unpleasant consequences so that threatening dangers for the "entire German nation" be averted. The action of the authorities against the Anabaptist reign in Münster, even as the action against the Anabaptist movement in general, was motivated by the argument of the disruption of public peace.[89] The estates wrote from Coblenz that the Anabaptists had risen up in arms against the Bishop, the cathedral chapter, and the knights of the chapter, had violently ousted the Bishop and the authority of the knights of the chapter, expelled the inhabitants of different beliefs, whose property they divided among themselves. They lived as they pleased, "in contrast to all rights of his Imperial Majesty and the public peace and order of the Empire."[90] Since keeping the public peace was the responsibility of the Empire, the estates of the Empire became involved. Citing the recess of the Diet of 1526, at first the nearest territories, then all territories were included in the military action and its financing. On June 25, 1535 the town was taken through treason and the bloody retribution began.

*   *   *

Let me, in closing, summarize my analysis of the position of the Anabaptist Kingdom of Münster within the tension between Anabaptism and imperial policy by stating two theses:

A. The Anabaptist Kingdom of Münster was not the inevitable consequence of Anabaptist theology, but a possible variant of the radical develop-

---

[87]Haus-, Hof- und Staatsarchiv Wien, Mainzer Erzkanzler-Archiv, Reichstagsakten, Nr. 6 c, fol. 132.

[88]Albert F. Mellink, *De wederdopers in de noordelijke nederlanden 1531-1544* (Leeuwarden, 1981); Idem, *Amsterdam en de wederdopers in de zestiende eeuw* (Nijmegen, 1978).

[89]Neuhaus, "Das Reich und die Wiedertäufer von Münster," 10ff.

[90]Stupperich, *Die Schriften Bernhard Rothmanns*, 413.

ment of Anabaptist thinking under the banner of the Apocalypse. It was an apocalyptically motivated alternative to the feudal political and social order which the Anabaptists rejected. It culminated in the attempt to realize the scriptural promise of a "new world" as the New Jerusalem before the Second Coming. In this respect the Anabaptist Kingdom was not a utopia, but an alternate social order which, however, proved not to be promising.

B. Since this alternative existed for a brief time and the old order in Münster was destroyed and new forms of rule were established, events acquired a fundamental political dimension. The threat to feudal rule was a challenge to feudal and municipal authorities. Since the counter-measures of the rulers were aimed at preventing the "entire German nation" from insurrection and at safeguarding the feudal order, the history of the Anabaptist Kingdom proved to be not only a local appearance in the Westphalian region but also a matter of imperial policy.

Detail from *Siege of Münster*,
woodcut by Erhard Schoen (*fl.* Nuremburg, 1525–50)

Christianity in One City:
Anabaptist Münster, 1534-35

James M. Stayer

Their learned teachers in Münster say that for fourteen hundred
years there have been no Christians on Earth.[1]

Jakob of Osnabrück

SINCE THE SIXTIES MÜNSTER ANABAPTISM has been the object of new
research that has made it less lurid and more intelligible by relating it more
successfully to the rest of Melchiorite Anabaptism, the other urban communal
reformations, and the politics of the Holy Roman Empire. This research has
more often than not concentrated on the preconditions of the Anabaptists
coming to power in Münster, but in the process added much to our grasp of
the Anabaptist regime itself. Its approach has been analytical and it has generally avoided moralizing rhetoric and facile comparisons with the bizarre sects
or totalitarian regimes of the twentieth century.[2] The outstanding recent
historian of Anabaptist Münster is Karl-Heinz Kirchhoff. He has challenged
both the traditional narrative and the traditional social stereotype about the
Münster Anabaptists. Whereas previously it was believed that the Anabaptists
took power when a weak Council lost control of lower class rabble, stirred up
by outside agitators, the Dutch prophets, Kirchhoff has argued that, instead,
a body of civic-minded notables of high social standing reluctantly sided with
the Anabaptists as the only means to preserve the endangered religious and
political freedoms of their city.[3]

The Münster Anabaptists were genuine Anabaptists, not a corrupt sect
misusing the Anabaptist name. The Anabaptist regime in Münster arose from
a peaceful Anabaptist movement established in the city since the summer of

---

[1]Joseph Niesert, ed., *Münsterische Urkundensammlung*, Vol. 1: *Urkunden zur Geschichte der
Münsterischen Wiedertäufer* (Coesfeld, 1826), 160; corrected in Carl Adolf Cornelius, ed., *Berichte
der Augenzeugen über das münsterische Wiedertäuferreich* (Münster, 1983, reprint of 1853 ed.), 417.
That this means there were no Christians before 1533, when Bernhard Rothmann and Jan
Matthijs of Haarlem revived Christianity in Münster and the Netherlands, is clarified elsewhere
in Rothmann's writings. See Robert Stupperich, ed., *Die Schriften Bernhard Rothmanns* (Münster,
1970), 217, 291-92, 354; James M. Stayer, *Anabaptists and the Sword* (Lawrence, Ks.: Coronado
Press, 1972), 247.

[2]See the contrasting treatments of Münster Anabaptism by Gerd Dethlefs and Robert
Stupperich, in *Die Wiedertäufer in Münster. Stadtmuseum Münster. Katalog der Eröffnungsausstellung*
(Münster, 1983), 19-36, 37-54.

[3]See especially Karl-Heinz Kirchhoff, *Die Täufer in Münster 1534/35* (Münster, 1973); idem,
"Gab es eine friedliche Täufergemeinde in Münster 1534?" *Jahrbuch des Vereins für westfälische
Kirchengeschichte* 55-56 (1963): 7-21. English translation by Elizabeth Bender, "Was there a Peace-
ful Anabaptist Congregation in Münster in 1534?" *Mennonite Quarterly Review* 44 (1970): 357-70.

1533, and its survivors and successors became peaceful Anabaptists after the fall of Münster, except for a militant remnant. What was typically Anabaptist was not violence or nonviolence but rejection of the wickedness of the world, as represented by the established church and government. The Swiss and South German Anabaptists, too, had oscillated between militance and social withdrawal when faced with the commoners' resistance movement in 1525.

What distinguished Münster Anabaptism was its link to a civic, communal Reformation led by Bernhard Rothmann, a non-Lutheran Reformer, at a time and in a region in which magisterial Reformation and conformity to Lutheran theology were politically inescapable. This unusual alliance between a communal Reformation and Anabaptism gave Münster Anabaptism its special power, but also assured its ultimate failure. It also accounts for the prominence in Anabaptist Münster of political notables and for authoritarian, elitist traits which make it less the commoners' Reformation than the religious radicalism of 1525 in South and Central Germany and Switzerland.

Melchiorite Anabaptism was a different Anabaptism. If the original Swiss Anabaptism originated in 1525 in the midst of the Peasants' War, and South German-Austrian Anabaptism arose in 1526 in the immediate aftermath of the crushing of the commoners' resistance, Melchiorite Anabaptism began in 1530 in Northern, Low German areas untouched by the events of 1525. Melchior Hoffman had been a radical lay preacher of the Reformation in the Baltic lands, shaped more by Wittenberg radicalism than by Luther.[4] In 1529 and 1530 he adopted the various forms of sacramental radicalism, including commitment to believers' baptism. More fateful were other heterodox positions he worked out in interaction with radical and prophetic circles in Strassburg: an idiosyncratic Christology focused on the divinity of Christ, a claim of personal charisma for himself as a messenger of the apocalypse, and the appointment of Strassburg as a city of refuge at the end of the world, which Hoffman had long set for 1533. In 1531 in response to the execution of some Dutch followers, Hoffman decreed a two-year suspension of baptism. Imprisoned in Strassburg in 1533, he predicted a theocratic interim kingdom in which a "revolution from above" would be conducted by a pious king instructed by a prophet. Together prophet and king would prepare the world for Christ's return, according to Hoffman's *Von der reinen Furcht Gottes*.[5] In the years before 1534 the Melchiorites were a significant sect but not a mass movement, chiefly centered in Strassburg, Münster, and the Netherlands. The focal importance of Melchior Hoffman for Anabaptism in Münster and the Nether-

---

[4]Calvin A. Pater, *Karlstadt as Father of the Baptist Movements: The Emergence of Lay Protestantism* (Toronto, 1984), 173-217.

[5]Klaus Deppermann, *Melchior Hoffman. Soziale Unruhen und apokalyptische Visionen* in *Zeitalter der Reformation* (Göttingen, 1979), 57-75, 194-235, 286.

lands is agreed upon by the in-group accounts of Obbe Philips and Nicolaas Blesdijk.[6]

The Reformation in Münster turned out to be a hothouse made to order for the expansion of Melchiorite Anabaptism. The political order in the city was legitimated by the communal will–the burghers regarded themselves as fellow citizens rather than subjects of the ruling Council. In normal times the Council ruled uncontested, but in times of popular excitement a long-established tradition gave the United Guild a right to veto actions of the Council. Furthermore, each year ten electors, directly elected by the full citizens, chose the twenty-four man Council. Normally the electors reconfirmed the councilors in office but in times of public discontent they could replace them.[7] In early 1533, not only were twenty of the Council members replaced at the time of the triumph of the Reformation, but a change of social caste occurred. The older group of political notables, whose families had traditionally sat in the Council, were replaced by a new group, of equal wealth but lesser status, who had earlier dominated the United Guild.[8] Communal power was a reality in the Münster Reformation; correspondingly the first Münster church ordinance of April 1533 made the radical proposal that preachers should be elected by their congregations.[9] But by the 1530s communal Reformations, typical in the 1520s, were an anachronism. In the aftermath of the Peasants' War city councils were assigned legal responsibility to maintain the public peace of the Empire. The Münster Council was continually torn between the communal vitality of the city's Reformation and its assigned role in the power constellation of the Holy Roman Empire.[10]

Externally Münster's Reformation was secured against the opposition of its overlord, the Prince Bishop, by the assistance of its powerful Lutheran neighbor, Philip of Hesse, the leader of the Schmalkaldic League. Due to the

[6]Obbe Philips, "Bekenntenisse," in *Bibliotheca Reformatoria Neerlandica*, ed. S. Cramer and F. Pijper (The Hague, 1910), 7, 121-38. English translation in G. H. Williams and Angel M. Mergal, eds., *Spiritual and Anabaptist Writers* (Philadelphia: Westminster, 1957), 206-25. Nicolaas Blesdijk, "Van den Oorspronck ende anvanck des sectes welck men wederdoper noomt," Universitätsbibliothek Basel, Jorislade X-4, described in S. Zijlstra, *Nicolaas Meyndertsz. van Blesdijk. Een bijdrage tot de geschiedenis van het Davidjorisme* (Assen, 1983), 149-53.

[7]Heinz Schilling, "Aufstandsbewegungen in der Stadtbürgerlichen Gesellschaft des Alten Reiches. Die Vorgeschichte des Münsteraner Täuferreiches, 1525-1534," in *Der Deutsche Bauernkrieg 1524-1526*, ed. H.-U. Wehler (Göttingen, 1975), 197-98, 213, 225, 230-33.

[8]Taira Kuratsuka, "Gesamtgilde und Täufer: Der Radikalisierungsprozess in der Reformation in Münster: Von der reformatorischen Bewegung zum Täuferreich 1533/34," *Archiv für Reformationsgeschichte* 76 (1985): 234-38, 263-65.

[9]Ibid., 238-39: "Eine so ausgeprägte Zuständigkeit des Volks eines Kirchspiels bei der Predigerwahl fand sich in dieser Zeit ausserhalb Münsters weder in den zwinglianischen Städten in Süddeutschland noch in den lutherischen Städten in Norddeutschland."

[10]Schilling, "Aufstandsbewegungen," 206, 218-19; Günther Vogler, "Das Täuferreich zu Münster als Problem der Politik im Reich," *Mennonitische Geschichtsblätter* 42 (1985): 7-23.

power of the League after its organization in 1531 the adherents of the Augsburg Confession enjoyed a *de facto* religious toleration. This was the basis of the political victory of the Münster Reformation, ratified by the Treaty of Dülmen, 14 February 1533.

It was Münster's ill fate, however, that its popular leading Reformer, Bernhard Rothmann, was an eclectic theologian, borrowing heavily from Swiss and South German sources.[11] The natural course of the Reformation in Münster, corresponding to its communal ethos and the theology of its leader, would have been Reformed.[12] However, at the time the Swiss Reformed were suffering from the loss of Zwingli and Oecolampadius, while the Strassburg theologians were working for a concord with Wittenberg. In the Empire, as opposed to Switzerland, an official non-Lutheran Reformation was impossible. The theologians of Marburg and Wittenberg tried to whip Rothmann and Münster into Lutheran orthodoxy, to which Rothmann responded by opening himself and the city progressively to Melchiorite influence.[13] The spearhead of the Münster Melchiorite movement were the Wassenberg preachers, led by Heinrich Roll, who arrived from Jülich in September 1532. In April 1533 the North German Lutheran theologians rejected the church ordinance of the Münster Reformation, sniffing "Sacramentarianism," and by the summer Rothmann had been won over by Wassenberger arguments to the further Melchiorite principle of believers' baptism. Jan of Leyden, the future Anabaptist king, visited Münster in the summer of 1533 because he had heard "that the Word of God was preached there best and most forcefully."[14]

The Münster Council and its Lutheran syndicus, Johan von der Wieck, were appalled that Rothmann had set Münster on a course towards imperial outlawry by violating the terms of the anti-Anabaptist Mandate of Speyer of 1529.[15] But the Lutheranism of the Münster Reformation did not go much deeper than *raison d'etat*. When the Council staged a debate on infant and adult baptism in August 1533 Rothmann was in public eyes the winner. Rothmann's radical religious development posed a dilemma for the "new notables" running the United Guild. The United Guild's communal role was

---

[11]Martin Brecht, "Die Theologie Bernhard Rothmanns," *Jahrbuch für Westfälische Kirchengeschichte* 78 (1985): 49-82; idem, "Die Ulmer Kirchenordnung von 1531, die Basler Reformationsordnung von 1529 und die Münsteraner Zuchtordnung von 1533," in *Niederlande und Nordwestdeutschland. Franz Petri zum 80. Geburtstag,* ed. Wilfried Ebbrecht and Heinz Schilling (Köln, 1983), 154-63.

[12]Willem J. de Bakker, "De vroege theologie van Bernhard Rothmann. De gereformeerde achtergrond van het Münsterse Doperrijk," *Doopsgezinde Bijdragen* Nr. 3 (1977): 9-20.

[13]Kuratsuka, "Gesamtgilde und Täufer," 240-48; Brecht, "Theologie Rothmanns," 64-65.

[14]Confession of 25 July 1535, in Cornelius, *Berichte,* 370.

[15]See Wieck's letter of 15 Nov. 1533, in *Das Täuferreich zu Münster, 1534-1535,* ed. Richard van Dülmen (Munich, 1974), 35-38. Here he repeatedly refers to Rothmann's followers as "Anabaptists," although adult baptisms had not yet begun in Münster.

to support Rothmann against the Council's moves to suppress and silence him, in view of his broad popular support. Nevertheless, it hesitated to break ranks with the members of its own estate now in control of the Council. A crisis in November 1533 led the Münster ruling elite in Council and United Guild to an unsatisfactory compromise, so as to avoid possible civil strife. Lutheran preachers from Hesse were called in to provide Münster with a respectable religious order, but Rothmann and his Melchiorite adherents continued to be tolerated in the city, in clear violation of Imperial law and to the official displeasure of both the Prince Bishop and Philip of Hesse.[16]

At that point at the end of 1533 Münster Anabaptism ignited Anabaptism in the Netherlands and set in motion the great religious, social, and political crisis that temporarily made a mass movement of the Melchiorite sect. Rothmann's *Confession of the Two Sacraments*, published in November, was a classic peaceful Anabaptist statement. The great eclectic Anabaptist theologian, Pilgram Marpeck, would recognize it as such when he made it the basis of his *Vermahnung* of 1542, the most fundamental statement of the Marpeck congregations.[17] When Heinrich Roll brought Rothmann's *Confession* to the Netherlands, Jan Matthijs responded by reinstituting the baptism of adults, thus making the Melchiorite sect once more unequivocally baptist, as it was to remain in its later Mennonite version (although not in its Davidite variant).[18] Jan Matthijs demanded and received total recognition and obedience as an apocalyptic messenger, moving the end of the world from Hoffman's 1533 to Easter 1534, by the apocalyptic number of three and one-half months.[19] Jan's baptizers introduced actual baptism of adult believers to Münster in January 1534; thus the adult baptisms marked a higher stage of the Melchiorite movement in Münster, not its beginning.[20]

Jan Matthijs' prediction of the end of the world gained mass credibility through a "political miracle," the deliverance of Münster to the Anabaptists in February. The Council, unable to suppress Rothmann's religious following, suffered a collapse of its own authority, so that the United Guild, especially one of the two aldermen, Heinrich Redecker, became the real power in the city. An Anabaptist or Anabaptist sympathizer, Redecker organized burgher

[16]Kuratsuka, "Gesamtgilde und Täufer," 246-54.

[17]Frank J. Wray, "The 'Vermahnung' of 1542 and Rothmann's 'Bekenntnisse,'" *Archiv für Reformationsgeschichte* 47 (1956): 243-51.

[18]Blesdijk, "Oorspronck," 16vo., 17ro.; Albert F. Mellink, "Das münsterische Täufertum und die Niederlande," *Jahrbuch für Westfälische Kirchengeschichte* 78 (1985): 14-15.

[19]Karl-Heinz Kirchhoff, "Die Endzeiterwartung der Täufergemeinde zu Münster 1534/35," *Jahrbuch für Westfälische Kirchengeschichte* 78 (1985): 24.

[20]Brecht, "Theologie Rothmanns," p. 66: "Die Infizierung mit melchioritisch- täuferischen Vorstellungen in Münster erfolgte zuerst bei den Predigern und ihrer Theologie. Das geschah bereits Monate vor der endgültigen Ankunft der niederländischen Täufer und bereitete diese vor."

resistance in the face of rumors in late January and early February, that the Bishop was about to attack the city, perhaps with the treasonable complicity of the Council. Redecker represented about half the new ruling group of 1533, which now gradually sided with the Anabaptists.[21] For them religious sympathy with Rothmann and his following was undoubtedly mixed with the motive of upholding civic independence and preserving the Münster Reformation against the Bishop.

The events of February 9-11, in which the previously nonviolent Anabaptists were instructed by their prophets to take arms, were for the Münster Anabaptists an experience of God's intervention in history, an otherwise inexplicable deliverance like that of the Israelites crossing through the Red Sea.[22] Confronted with the armed supporters of the Council, still a majority in the city, now reinforced by a peasant military levy brought into Münster, and with the Bishop on his way with an armed escort, the Anabaptists thought of themselves as sheep for the slaughter.[23] The days of crisis, marked by unusual meteorological phenomena,[24] ended with a compromise that secured power in Münster to the pro-Anabaptist half of the ruling group. Redecker and the United Guild organized the election of an Anabaptist Council on February 23. Jan Matthijs moved to Münster and proclaimed it the divinely appointed city of refuge in the final tribulations. Letters and emissaries from Münster to the Melchiorites in Westphalia and the Netherlands declared the political miracle of February 1534 to be a literal miracle.

Jan Matthijs, until his death on Easter 1534, enjoyed an uncontested charismatic authority that far surpassed Hoffman's and that of all alter Melchiorite leaders.[25] Responding to the events in Münster, a wave of apocalyptic excitement swept over all estates in Westphalia and the Netherlands. (To try a modern analogy, image that you just learned that some wildly improbable group had come to power—not the African National Congress in Pretoria or the P.L.O. in Jerusalem, relatively rational possibilities—but perhaps that the Baader-Meinhof group had seized power in Bonn.)

The apocalyptic mood was climaxed by the attempts at mass immigration to Münster in March 1534. That prior conditions in the Netherlands in the thirties contributed a high level of latent social excitability is undeniable. This

---

[21]Kuratsuka, "Gesamtgilde und Täufer," 253-62.

[22]Ibid., 261: "Das Wunder 'beweist' den Täufern überzeugend, dass gerade Münster die Stadt des Herrn und das Neue Jerusalem sei. Das 'Wunder' wurde auch ihnen zum Urerlebnis wie es das Wunder im Roten Meer für das Volk Israel wurde."

[23]Kirchhoff, "Friedliche Täufergemeinde," provides the most satisfactory interpretation of 9-11 February 1534.

[24]Kirchhoff, "Endzeiterwartung," 31-37.

[25]See Otthein Rammstedt, *Sekte und soziale Bewegung. Soziologische Analyse der Täufer in Münster* (Köln and Opladen, 1966), 62-63, 68-86.

was a time of war, pestilence and unemployment,[26] just as the apocalyptic sections of the Bible had foretold that tribulations would be a sign of the last times. However, it does not seem to have been the case that the Münster Anabaptists' appeal, containing the promise that the immigrants' needs would be provided for, made the journey to Münster into a poor people's crusade. Kirchhoff's studies of Anabaptism in Coesfeld and Warendorf, major sources of the Westphalian immigration, indicate that a social cross-section of the population participated.[27] Henrich Gresbeck, author of the major eyewitness account of Anabaptist Münster, wrote that the newcomers had left their possessions behind, and that there were rich people among them.[28] Barend Dirks, a contemporary painter, depicting the migration of Netherlanders in the Amsterdam City Hall, described one of his paintings with the caption: "They sold jewels and clothes, land and property, in every nook and corner; hurrying on board ship with great desire, prophesying the quest for a new God."[29]

Most of the thousands who set out for Münster in March 1534 did not get there, but submitted passively to disbandment with confiscation of their money and arms. Released by authorities horrified at their numbers, they became the object of later appeals from Münster and formed the rank-and-file of later militant actions in support of Münster, like the seizure of Oldeklooster and the attack on the Amsterdam City Hall in the spring of 1535.[30] Blesdijk, like later historians, commented that the peaceful dispersion of the trekkers showed that they were moved more by apocalyptic excitement than genuine militancy.[31] On the other hand, there seems to have been no opposition to the trek within Melchiorite circles. Figures like Jan Matthijs of Middelberg and Jacob van Campen, who showed independence towards the later Münster leadership, probably participated.[32] In fact, the trekkers of March 1534 provided the basic membership pool for Dutch Anabaptism, at least for the duration of its militant phase.

However, Münster's unquestioned legitimacy among Melchiorites lasted only until Easter 1534, the predicted end of the world. During the first period of the siege, until Easter, Jan Matthijs exercised absolute authority in Münster,

---

[26]Mellink, *De Wederdopers in de Noordelijke Nederlanden, 1531-1544* (Groningen, 1954), 1-19.

[27]Kirchhoff, "Die Täufer in Münsterland," *Westfälische Zeitschrift* 113 (1963): 23.

[28]Gresbeck, in Cornelius, *Berichte*, 38, 51, 70.

[29]W. J. Kühler, "Anabaptism in the Netherlands," *The Anabaptists and Thomas Müntzer*, ed. Werner O. Packull and James M. Stayer (Dubuque, Iowa: Kendall-Hunt, 1980), 99-100.

[30]Lammert G. Jansma, "De chiliastische beweging der Wederdopers (1530-1535)," *Doopsgezinde Bijdragen* NR 5 (1979), 41-55, esp. 53.

[31]Zijlstra, Blesdijk, 155; Kühler, "Anabaptism," 98-100.

[32]Mellink, *Wederdopers*, 373.

overawing the elected Council and figures like Redecker who had put the Anabaptists in power.[33] When the prophesied supernatural deliverance did not come, Jan sallied out against the besieging army and, in effect, committed suicide on Easter, April 5, 1534.[34] His death left his followers trapped within Münster, doomed to cope with his prophetic failure as best they could.

Jan of Leyden never regained Jan Matthijs' legitimacy and authority. He called into question Münster's status as the New Jerusalem by toying with the idea of abandoning the city for an armed invasion of the Netherlands. Some militant Dutch Melchiorites, frustrated by King Jan's ineptness as a prophet, reacted to the failure of his prediction that Münster would be delivered before Easter 1535 by setting up a new Promised David in Jan van Batenburg.[35] Now some voices, Obbe Philips and perhaps David Joris, questioned Münster's turn from the peaceful path of Melchior Hoffman. This doubtful legitimacy accounts for the weakness of the Netherlands uprisings of 1535 in support of Münster, especially the attack on the Amsterdam City Hall in May.

Certainly in the Netherlands the Münsterite movement was in decline after April 1534. In besieged Münster a series of careful power-sharing arrangements were made between the immigrants and the local notables who had cooperated in the Anabaptists' taking power.[36] This was the reality behind the appearance of absolute power vested in King Jan. The result was an erosion of the strict community of goods instituted by Jan Matthijs. Community of goods and polygamy—the distinctive institutions of royal Anabaptist Müntzer, as they were practiced, became chiefly responses to the siege and the connected refugee problem. The reality of community of goods in Münster was nothing like the egalitarian transformation of patterns of life and work achieved by the Hutterites.[37] Although Münsterite polygamy reflected the broad interest among Reformation radicals in a regenerate sexuality, according to I Corinthians 7:29, its reality was the officering of the female majority according to the prescriptions of Biblical misogyny.[38] There was a lot of desperate playacting in Münster from the actor-king downward. These people must have recognized with one side of their minds after the failure of Jan Matthijs' prophecy that they were destined to violent death, a holy holocaust as

[33]For example, the execution without due process of the smith Hubert Ruescher. See Hermann von Kerssenbroch, *Anabaptistici furoris . . .* in *Die Geschichtsquellen des Bisthums Münster* 5, ed. Heinrich Detmer (Münster, 1900), 559-61.

[34]Kirchhoff, "Endzeiterwartung," 39.

[35]Jansma, "Chiliastische beweging," passim.

[36]Kirchhoff, *Täufer in Münster*, 68-77.

[37]H.-D. Plümper, *Die Gütergemeinschaft bei den Täufern des 16. Jahrhunderts* (Göppingen, 1972), 186.

[38]James M. Stayer, "Vielweiberei als 'innerweltliche Askese'. Neue Eheauffassungen in der Reformationszeit," *Mennonitische Geschichtsblätter* 37 (1980): 24-41.

Rothmann put it in one of his last writings.[39] In the meantime, the privileges of notables over commoners and of men over women continued.

Kirchhoff's prosopographical study of Anabaptist property-holders native to Münster, based on records of Anabaptist property confiscated following the Bishop's conquest of the city, shows an astonishing normality in distribution of wealth among the Münster Anabaptists. The social structure of the Anabaptist property-holders turned out to be very similar both to that of post-Anabaptist Münster and to the comparable city of Hildesheim. In other words, a random sample of the Münster property-owners chose Anabaptism rather than Lutheranism or Catholicism in the Reformation crisis of 1532-35.[40] Kirchhoff arrived at a similar result by contrasting the Anabaptist ruling elite with the Anabaptist rank and file. Despite the introduction of community of goods, persons who had been rich property-owners in the old order were represented in disproportionate numbers among the political leaders of the new regime.[41] There was, indeed, a silent majority of the poor and of women in besieged Anabaptist Münster, but rather than being "the real carriers of Anabaptism,"[42] they were victims of the regime.

Anabaptist Münster was conquered in June 1535 after sixteen months of resistance, including the defeat of two assaults in May and late August 1534. The Bishop was able to continue the costly siege only with extensive financial aid from the Empire, justified by the threat that the Anabaptists allegedly posed to the public peace.[43] In the eyes of their enemies at least the Münster Anabaptists continued the commoners' rebellion of 1525.

Until the fall of Münster internal Melchiorite critique of the Anabaptist state was scattered and muted. With the end of the Anabaptist resistance, however, the distinctive Münsterite practices such as the militant premillenial Kingdom and the polygamous marriage of the saints came quickly into dispute. At Bocholt in August 1536 the victor's palm went to David Joris,[44] a new promised David who could obscure the disputed issues through spiritualization. The Davidite sect became increasingly Nicodemite, eventually abandoning a distinctive baptismal practice. In the 1540's Menno Simons became the paramount leader of the Melchiorite remnant, now dwindled from

---

[39]Stupperich, *Die Schriften Bernhard Rothmanns*, 441-42: "Wol an dan, zo wi . . . moethen ock under den voithen des beestes verstampeth werdenn, gevelt idt Godt also, so wyllen wi myt allen hilligen verdult dregen."

[40]Kirchhoff, *Täufer in Münster*, 35-44, esp. 42: "die Sozialstruktur der Täufer sich nicht wesentlich von der eines zufälligen Ausschnitts aus der Gesamtbürgerschaft unterscheidet."

[41]Ibid., 77.

[42]This is the view of Kuratsuka, "Gesamtgilde und Täufer," 266-68.

[43]Vogler, "Täuferreich," 7ff.

[44]James M. Stayer, "David Joris: A Prolegomenon to Further Research," *Mennonite Quarterly Review* 59 (1985): 350-61.

mass movement to sect, by radically toning down their apocalyptic expectations and focusing their inner-worldly asceticism on sober conduct, tempered only by the ecstasy of martyrdom. Yet Menno's Melchiorite Anabaptism contained sectarian distinctives, setting it apart from the groups in South Germany and Switzerland. It had more theological content, concerns like the Melchiorite Christology, while the Swiss Brethren religion was almost exhausted in *Ordnungen*, rules of conduct.[45] The Swiss Brethren most radically expressed the leveling, laicizing impulse of the early Reformation, while the greater authority of Mennonite elders over their flock seems to have been a watered-down continuation of the charisma of the early Melchiorite prophets.

The reinterpretation of Münster Anabaptism here described has decided relevance for our view of Münster's ambitious experiment with community of goods. Community of goods among Anabaptists in North Germany and the Netherlands was obviously not a direct and immediate result of the events of 1525, neither the commoners' resistance and its suppression, nor the wave of believers' baptisms spreading from Zurich. Melchior Hoffman had contacts with various Strassburg radicals, including Anabaptists, in the early thirties,[46] but he was no mere transmitter of High German influences to the different milieux of Lower Germany.

It now seems reasonable to distinguish three phases of the Melchiorite movement in Münster. The first extends from the summer of 1533, when Rothmann adopted the radical sacramental position of the Wassenbergers, to February 1534. During this period the Melchiorite movement was powerful, perhaps the most powerful religious current among the Münster commoners, but it still lacked official sanction and it still responded to its opponents with peaceful avoidance. From February 1534, with its "political miracles," to Easter of that year, Anabaptist Münster was at the focal point of an apocalyptic crisis which legitimated the prophetic authority of Jan Matthijs. Militancy and radical community of goods corresponded to this crisis. From April 1534 to the fall of the Anabaptist regime in June 1535 Münster's apocalyptic enthusiasm was in decline, but at the same time desperate efforts were made to preserve the energies and idealism of the earlier period under the inventive, institution-building leadership of Jan of Leyden. Rammstedt's concept of "the institutionalization of charisma" does, after all, despite its reserved reception by other scholars, seem a good description of what occurred in Münster after the disappointment with Jan Matthijs' prophecy.[47] Community of goods now was shaped increasingly by the military necessities of the siege and by the need

[45]John S. Oyer, "The Strasbourg Conferences of the Anabaptists," *Mennonite Quarterly Review* 58 (1984): 218-29.

[46]Deppermann, *Melchior Hoffman*, 139-93.

[47]Rammstedt, *Sekte*, 74-83, esp. 74: "Eine verfehlte Prophetie bewirkt nicht das Ende der chiliastischen Bewegung, aber die charismatische Herrschaft schlägt um in Institution und Dogma."

to appease a leadership group in which notables were prominent. Richard van Dülmen goes so far as to assert that, although community of goods was the declared goal of Münster's preachers and prophets, "it was only partially achieved and later even partially abolished."[48]

Community of goods was part of the stock of ideas of Bernhard Rothmann as Reformer of Münster. In his first Anabaptist writing, *The Confession of the Two Sacraments*, Rothmann connected community of goods with the Christian solidarity of the Lord's Supper, in which the communicants are one body, one bread. Here Rothmann explicitly cited the *Chronica* of Sebastian Franck, where Franck uses the apocryphal Fourth Epistle of Clement to show that property arose among Christians from the bishops' betrayal of their trust:

> The Bishop and his servants, the deacons, were common householders and stewards, not only in the spirit but for physical needs. They parceled out all common goods according to everyone's needs. They then started to become avaricious, to turn common goods into private property and to appropriate it for themselves.[49]

Franck, of course, was no Anabaptist, but his writings enjoyed great authority in the Netherlands among Melchiorites and later among Mennonites. His anti-authoritarian profiles of sacred and profane history conveyed among Northerners the viewpoints of High German Reformation radicalism. In the section that Rothmann cited Franck digressed from discussing the Lord's Supper to treat of the origins of property. "In justice everything should be common," wrote Franck. Property, like dominion, began with the usurpation of the wicked Nimrod after the Flood. Not only Acts 2 but Plato and Epicurus witness against it.

No doubt Sebastian Franck's ideal of a communist golden age in the past helped to shape Münster Anabaptists' reaction to the apocalyptic crisis which began in February 1534. But that crisis was dominated by another spirit less inclusive and tolerant than Franck's. Jan Matthijs called for the carrying out of God's will immediately and without compromise. The godless must be expelled from Münster without delay, leaving their property behind. Jan Matthijs personally commanded that, since property was abolished and all goods were now common to everyone, there should be an immediate conflagration of "letters and seals, as well as privileges, registers and all other books and accounts."[50] This wave of expulsion and destruction aimed at total purification. All things were to become new in the twinkling of an eye.

[48]Richard van Dülmen, *Reformation als Revolution* (Munich, 1977), 307.

[49]Stupperich, *Die Schriften Bernhard Rothmanns*, 184-85; Sebastian Franck, *Chronica, Zeytbuch und Geschychtbibel* (Strassburg, 1536), 244.

[50]Confession of Jan of Leyden, 25 July 1535, in Cornelius, *Berichte*, 374.

One of the few glimpses we have of the practice of the peaceful separatist congregation before the arrival of Jan Matthijs comes from Jakob Hufschmidt from Osnabrück, who left Münster about the time Jan got there, late in February 1534. Answering questions during an interrogation, he affirmed that the Anabaptists taught that usury and *interest* contracts were unchristian. They were not to be extracted by Anabaptists from others, nor were they to be paid by the Anabaptists themselves. The congregation had two officers concerned with the care of the poor. These reported cases of need, received voluntary contributions, and administered poor relief.[51]

Certainly the significant exchange of populations that took place in Münster in February and March 1534, when about two thousand non-Anabaptists were expelled and about twenty-five hundred Anabaptists immigrated into the city,[52] was an important determining factor in the practice of community of goods. Both in Moravia and in Münster the radical practice of community of goods was connected with a refugee problem. The population exchange, of course, followed Jan Matthijs' prophetic script, which demanded both the extirpation of the godless and the ingathering of the regenerate in the few weeks of grace that remained before the end of the world. Something similar would have occurred anyhow, because no early modern city tolerated hostile elements during a siege, and because outside Münster persecution by the governments and flight by the Anabaptists were the predictable outcomes of the twist Jan Matthijs had given to the Melchiorite movement.

The appeal for Anabaptist immigration has usually been presented by historians as directed to the poor and unemployed, "There is sufficient provision for the saints," the trekkers were assured. Of course, in the next phrase the newcomers are instructed to bring money, as well as food and clothing for the journey.[53] Rothmann's letter to Heinrich Slachtschaf, commanding him to bring the Anabaptist congregation in Coesfeld to Münster, shows how little the March appeals singled out the poor: "The Lord witnessed to us through his prophets that the saints are to be gathered into this city. Therefore they ordered me to write to you that you should tell the brothers to get here promptly, bringing with them the money, gold and silver that they have on hand; the rest of their goods they should hand over to the sisters, who should dispose of it and follow."[54] In the apocalyptic moment there were to be no rich or poor, no men or women; but in the provisional haven in Münster it appears that men with money were at a premium!

[51]Niesert, *Urkundensammlung*, 161-62, 164.

[52]Kirchhoff, *Täufer in Münster*, 24.

[53]J. de Hullu, ed., *Bescheiden betreffende de Hervorming in Overijssel*, Vol. 1: *Deventer (1522-1546)* (Deventer, 1899), 153-54.

[54]Stupperich, *Die Schriften Bernhard Rothmanns*, 51.

However that may be, it cannot be denied that in the beginning of Anabaptist Münster, women and poor people responded with enthusiasm to its community of goods. A woman from Münster wrote to her sister outside, requesting that her daughter be sent to join her in Münster: "I'm not concerned whether she has clothes or not. Send her to me; she'll have enough here. For you should know that the Almighty has bestowed such grace upon us that I am able to go about in gold velvet and silk clothes. . . . And the poorest have become as rich through God's grace as the burghermasters or magistrates of the city."[55]

The reordering of property arrangements seems to have begun with Jan Matthijs' preaching that the possessions of the emigrès should belong in common to those who remained. He organized the storing of household furnishings and clothing in appointed houses, as well as the destruction of deeds and the confiscation of valuables.[56] Jan Matthijs never changed Münster's institutional structure, unlike his successor Jan of Leyden. His authority was personal and indirect; so the actual promulgation of community of goods came from a consensus of the prophets, preachers and Council.[57] Rothmann preached that "everything Christian brothers and sisters have belongs to one as well as the other. You will lack nothing—whether goods, clothing or house and home. You will receive whatever you need. God won't allow you to go wanting. Everything will be common. It belongs to all of us."[58]

Specifically this decision of the Council involved a call for all residents of Münster to surrender their money and precious metals. According to Gresbeck there was a good deal of resistance and delay in compliance with this decree. The enforcement dragged on for two months, past Jan Matthijs' death, and involved some exemplary executions for noncompliance.[59]

Later in the year, writing his *Restitution*, Rothmann summed up the actual accomplishments of community of goods in Münster as the abolition of "buying and selling, working for money, and indebtedness and usury."[60] This equated community of goods with the abolition of a money economy. Gresbeck described the anti-money rhetoric of the Anabaptist leaders in the

---

[55]Getrud from Münster, 18 March 1534, cited in Rammstedt, *Sekte*, 90.

[56]Kerssenbroch, in Detmer, *Die Geschichtsquellen*, 556-58.

[57]Gresbeck, in *Berichte*, 32: "Demnach hebben die propheten, predicanten und der gantze raet tho rade gegain, und wolden al guet gemein hebben." Seemingly this is contradicted by Knipperdollinck, confession of 21 Jan. 1536, in ibid., 410: "Er sagt, Johan Mathis, der Kuningk und predicanten haven gemeinschoft der guder ingefurt, und er nit." Certainly the Council and burghermasters legitimated the abolition of property, even if the idea did originally come from the prophets and preachers.

[58]Gresbeck, ibid.

[59]Gresbeck, ibid., 33.

[60]Stupperich, *Die Schriften Bernhard Rothmanns*, 256.

following terms: "They said that they were Christians, that a Christian should have no money, that it was totally unclean for Christians, that Christians should not buy and sell from each other but should barter, and that throughout the whole world the one city should barter with the other."[61] Enforcing a "natural" economy based on barter corresponded to the social idealism of the time, as we are reminded when we read Thomas More's description of how things were done in Utopia. Gresbeck's suggestion that there was talk about abolishing money throughout the world suits the temper of the end-time expectations aroused by Jan Matthijs. However, unlike documents of indebtedness, which were destroyed, money and precious metals were collected at the City Council's chancellery.[62] Again, the practice of the Münster government was like that in Utopia—the common store of money and valuables was used for dealing with outsiders, to pay for imports, and to conduct military operations.

The executors of community of goods in Münster were the deacons. The meaning of community there was contained in, and circumscribed by, the tasks of these officers. The number of the deacons is one of many matters on which our sources conflict. Kerssenbrock refers to seven deacons, whom he mentions by name (four or five of whom Kirchhoff has identified as natives of Münster), while Gresbeck writes of three deacons in each parish, or eighteen all together.[63]

Deacons preserved and distributed the goods of emigrés chiefly to assist immigrants, but in principle to aid all needy members of the community. The cloisters, emptied and plundered immediately after the election of the Anabaptist Council, were used to accommodate newcomers, and so, apparently, were deserted houses.[64] The deacons also supervised common meals for the watch and for workers of both sexes repairing the walls and trenches. These meals were served at a community house, one located near each of the ten gates. One deacon supervised the food procurement for each of the ten community houses.[65]

The deacons in each parish were commissioned to make an inventory of personal possessions, food, household goods and clothing, and to redistribute excess supplies to the needy poor. Gresbeck noted that after two or three visitations this practice fell into abeyance for the time, because in the early stages of the siege no one went hungry. He also observed that not everyone revealed everything he had to the deacons.[66]

[61]Gresbeck, in *Bericht*, 48-49.

[62]Kerssenbroch, in Detmer, *Die Geschichtsquellen*, 558.

[63]Kerssenbroch, ibid.; Kirchhoff, *Täufer in Münster*, 69; Gresbeck, in Cornelius, *Berichte*, 34.

[64]Kerssenbroch, in Detmer, *Die Geschichtsquellen*, 541-42, 558; Gresbeck, in Cornelius, *Berichte*, 165.

[65]Gresbeck, ibid., 34-35.   [66]Gresbeck, ibid.

Under Jan Matthijs a community of goods had been introduced that variously affected different kinds of property. Money, precious metals and jewels were, in theory at least, removed from private possession and made into a public utility. All movable possessions, houses and property of emigrès were confiscated, some made available to immigrants, some preserved in public stores or otherwise kept in the control of the deacons and government. The movable and immovable property of Münster residents who did not flee in February (estimated by Kirchhoff as two-thirds of the population of Anabaptist Münster[67]) was only touched to the extent that it was inventoried and in principle made available for poor relief. For the time there was no attempt to interfere with the Münster residents' possession of their houses. Such a state of affairs preserved many of the natural advantages of Münster residents, particularly the more prosperous of them centered among the "new notables" who had earlier helped the Anabaptists to power.

Still, during the first prophet's six weeks of ascendancy a tremendous upheaval of property relations had occurred, money had been abolished as a medium of internal exchange and the principle of economic equality had been announced. However, the patriarchal household continued as the primary unit of production and consumption—later confirmed in this function by household-centered polygamous marriage—and there was no practicable method to put all households on the same level of well-being. Both the absolute rigor of Jan Matthijs' acts and the hit-or-miss quality of the results were conditioned by his belief that the time was very short. For him it was.

Jan of Leyden had the unenviable task of trying to stabilize Anabaptist Münster on the morrow of the realization that the apocalypse had not come, at least not when and how it was expected. He played Niccolo Machiavelli's ultimate political role— that of the giver of laws and shaper of institutions, not once but twice, in creating the regime of the Twelve Elders and his own kingship. The theatrical effects of the career of the actor-tailor-prophet-king have often been noted, usually without appreciation of his necessary political tasks, to maintain apocalyptic enthusiasm among the rank-and-file of the besieged, and to integrate the two political elites of his realm, the Münster notables and the immigrant Melchiorites. Six of the Twelve Elders were former Council members in Münster. Of the 148 official members of King Jan's court, about half came from Münster and 25 of them were former office-holders. The former office-holders became more numerous the more prominent the position at court.[68] Burghermaster Bernd Knipperdollinck acted, in effect, as vice-

[67]Kirchhoff, *Täufer in Münster*, 24.

[68]Ibid., 68-77, esp. 77: "auch in der Täufergemeinde, wo es nach Einführung der Gütergemeinschaft theoretisch keine Vermögensunterschiede gab, konnten die wolhhabenden Vertreter der früheren städtischen Führungsschicht in beträchtlicher Anzahl zu Rang, Ansehen und Einfluß gelangen."

regent for Jan both under the Elders and in the Kingdom. How important he was considered is shown by his restoration to office after his aborted attempt to gain popular support to set up his own, "spiritual" kingship.[69]

In one of the early decrees of the Twelve Elders Jan of Leyden gave explicit recognition to a right of inheritance which had, presumably, never been interrupted in Anabaptist Münster. The administrator of inheritances was to be none other than Knipperdollinck.[70] The creation of the royal court gave rise to an ostentatious, privileged minority, especially offensive in the bitter, hungry last months of the siege.[71] Towards the end the rulers put women, children and old men who couldn't fight on starvation rations, at the same time disingenuously permitting them to leave the city and expose themselves to the brutalities of the besieging mercenary army.[72] Gresbeck, who, we must remember, went over to the enemy at the end, insisted that community of goods in Anabaptist Münster was ultimately fraudulent: "But whoever was poor stayed poor. The person who had something was able to draw on it at the end, despite the fact that goods were supposed to be common. So hunger first afflicted the poor people, who suffered great misery."[73]

On the other hand, under the Kingdom, with the greater severity of the siege, a kind of war rationing was imposed. Both Gresbeck and Kerssenbroch describe a great collection of both clothing and food from the houses shortly after the proclamation of the Kingdom.[74] This collection was connected with an attempt to prescribe limits on the amount of clothing any individual was allowed. Gresbeck describes what occurred as more a collection of stores for the Dutch newcomers and for the court than a genuine assistance of the needy. His bias, of course, was to present most of what occurred in Münster as a swindle for the benefit of the newly powerful Dutch immigrants. Such an interpretation has to be strongly modified by Kirchhoff's evidence of the continuing prominence of Münster residents in the Anabaptist ruling group[75]—but, in fact,

---

[69]Gresbeck, in Cornelius, *Berichte*, 149-50; Kerssenbroch, in Detmer, *Die Geschichtsquellen*, 690-95.

[70]Kerssenbroch, in Detmer, *Die Geschichtsquellen*, 586: "si quis Deo dispensante ab hostibus transfossus aut alia quavis ratione obdormierit in Domino, bona illius relicta, ut sunt arma, vestes etc., nemo sua auctoritate capiet, sed ad Bernardum Knipperdollingum ensigerum deferentur, qui senioribus ea offeret, ut illorum auctoritate veris haeredibus adiudicentur."

[71]Gresbeck, 86-89, esp. 88: "So heft sick der konningk ouck so kostlick gerust mit seinen dieners. Und dat iss al des Vaders wille gewest, dat hei sick so rusten sol, wante der konigh sachte, hei wer dem fleisch afgestorven und hedde dair gein homoit mede, und dede dat Gode tho eheren. . . . Mehr der gemein man en konde nicht wieder krigen von seinem gelt ofte von seinem silver oder golt, aver der konigh und die rede droegent und heddent under handen. Dieser konigh und predicanten plagen dat volck tho seggen, dat sie nicht na dem fleisch und na der welt solden leven, und in den menschen sol anders nicht sein dan der geist. . . ."

[72]Ibid., 172-73.

[73]Ibid., 69.

[74]Ibid., 96-97; Kerssenbroch, in Detmer, *Die Geschichtsquellen*, 638-39.

[75]Kirchhoff, *Täufer in Münster*, 68-77.

perhaps half of the ruling group *were* outsiders newly raised to prominence in Münster, like Jan of Leyden himself.

At this same time early in the Kingdom official admonitions were made for those with the more spacious houses to be prepared to accommodate guests from the outside. Münster's hopes for deliverance were fastened on a massive, militant migration of Anabaptists from the surrounding territories. Gresbeck's account continued that the king and his councilors intended a general exchange of dwellings "so that the foreigners would have the best houses in the city." But "the common people or burghers weren't willing. True, a part of the burghers were willing and moved out of their houses into better ones. Otherwise everyone who wanted remained in his own house."[76] Here again King Jan was capable of acknowledging limits to his power in a way Jan Matthijs never did, except when he allowed himself to be taken out of an actual slaughter of non-Anabaptists in February. The houses of the Münster residents, which the Anabaptist leadership sniffed at, then backed away from, were the chief remainder of unexpended wealth available to the Bishop after the conquest.[77] The records of these confiscated houses and properties form the basis for Kirchhoff's study of the social composition of Anabaptist Münster.

Towards the end of the siege, war communism in Münster amounted not so much to confiscation of property, although house searches were frequent enough and vacant plots of ground were expropriated and put under cultivation,[78] as a dole to the hungry from government stores. The government used its treasure in the months before the city was entirely cut off from the outside to buy beer and flour and horses and cows. The last major task of the deacons was to visit the houses and distribute minimum rations according to the number of enumerated persons in each house.[79] The deacons' administration of community of goods, like everything else in the sixteen months of Anabaptist Münster, was determined by the siege.

Curiously, as the reality of Münster's communism was eroded, its dogmatic expression in Rothmann's writings was continually polished and sharpened. This same generalization applies to his apocalyptic writing.[80] When apocalyptic hopes were at their peak early in 1534 Rothmann composed a merely legalistic defense of the Münster government, as engaged

---

[76]Gresbeck, 97-98.

[77]Kirchhoff, *Täufer in Münster*, 4: "Bischof Franz ließ später dazu erklären, die Beute sei nicht groß gewesen. . . . Das in Münster vorhandene Geld hätten die Täufer für ihre Werbungen im Ausland verbraucht." In the end the Bishop was able to touch only 13-16 percent of the value of the confiscated houses because of the high burden of previous debt weighing upon them. (Ibid., 7-8).

[78]Gresbeck, 140-41, 175-76.

[79]Ibid., 174.

[80]See Rammstedt, *Sekte*, 83-86.

in justified resistance to a tyrannical overlord. This was the substance of the *Confession of the Faith and Life of the Congregation of Christ in Münster*. By the time Rothmann hit the high apocalyptic pitch of *On Vengeance* in late 1534 the apocalyptic faith was on the wane, outside Münster anyhow, as the tract indirectly acknowledged. In his *Restitution* Rothmann proclaimed that the Anabaptist realm had abolished human exploitation: "the eating and drinking of the sweat of the poor, that is, to use our servants and our neighbors, so that they must work so that we may feast."[81]

In practice Anabaptist communism in Münster fell far short of Rothmann's ideal. It reached its high point in the heady weeks following the "February miracle." Afterward it showed its tawdry reality as a dreary "war communism," modified and made still more unappealing by King Jan's responsiveness to the elite of notables who had put the Anabaptists in charge of Münster to begin with. The wheel of historical fashion has turned against saying that the peasants' and commoners' goals were unrealizable in 1525, but it still seems incontestable that the Münsterites were foredoomed to failure, because of the "reality loss" inherent in their apocalyptic worldview. No doubt, Anabaptist Münster could not have succeeded on the North German plain in 1535 in its specific social and political constellation. But hardly a hundred years previously another apocalyptic trek to a place of refuge had generated a political and military power of substance at Tabor in southern Bohemia. Had Jan of Leyden's resistance succeeded, communism in Anabaptist Münster would surely have been discarded, just as it was at Tabor.

---

[81]Stupperich, *Die Schriften Bernhard Rothmanns*, 256.

Index

Index compiled by Paula Presley

About the Contributors

Eric W. Gritsch is Professor of Church History and Director of the Institute for Luther Studies at the Lutheran Theological Seminary in Gettysburg, Pennyslvania, U.S.A.

Hans J. Hillerbrand is Professor of History and Religious Studies at Southern Methodist University in Dallas, Texas, U.S.A.

Siegfried Hoyer is Professor of History at Karl Marx Universität in Leipzig, German Democratic Republic.

Adolf Laube is Professor of History at the Akademie der Wissenschaften der DDR, Zentralinstitut für Geschichte, Berlin, German Democratic Republic.

Sigrid Looß is associated with the Akademie der Wissenschaften der DDR, Zentralinstitut für Geschichte, Berlin, German Democratic Republic.

James M. Stayer is Professor of History at Queen's University in Kingston, Ontario, Canada.

Günter Vogler is Professor of History at Humboldt Universität in Berlin, German Democratic Republic.

DATE DUE

APR 1 3 '89		
DEC 1 7 '90		
APR 1 5 1992		
MAY 2 1 2003		
5/31/13		